MW01531953

You bought this book because you want to change your life. In your mind you think it is about making money. Nothing could be further from the truth. You have a sense of adventure about yourself and this is a chance to do something you have always wanted to do, be your own person and if you want it bad enough that is exactly what will happen. The information in this book is applicable to many different businesses, so for you my friend the sky is the limit. v

Wishing you the best!

Glendon Cameron

5.0 out of 5 stars **Excellent Advice From Someone Who Is Successful**
This book is current, unlike others, and offers sound advice for people new to the business as well as experienced unit buyers.**Read more**

Published 3 months ago by rjdavid1

5.0 out of 5 stars **Worth it...**
I bought the ebook (cheaper) from Glendon's website. After watching several of his YouTube videos, he seemed like a good guy and a straight-shooter. **Read more**

Published 4 months ago by Jeff Snavely

4.0 out of 5 stars **Good Book - It will get you started**
I purchased this book and "Buy for a dollar Sell for Two" about storage unit auctions. There are a lot a stories and useful info in this book. **Read more**

Published 4 months ago by Big Dave

5.0 out of 5 stars **A money maker**
This book is an easy read and I did it in 1 day. Having run a small online business for a few years now and just getting into the storage unit auction business (I have attended... **Read more**

Published 5 months ago by astainless

5.0 out of 5 stars **Best self help book yet, isn't it?**
This is the best SELF HELP book out there. If you read it and put it to use, then you can't be anything else but helped. Get it, read it and help yourself! **Read more**

Published 5 months ago by InsaneCardPlayer

5.0 out of 5 stars **making money a-z with storage unit auctions**
If you are looking to make money from storage unit auctions, then this is the book for you. I have followed Glendon's blogs for over 6 months, and purchased the book about 4... **Read more**

5.0 out of 5 stars **Money well spent!!!!**
This book has a lot of useful tips and information for a beginner like me. I have read the book twice in a four day period.**Read more**

Published 7 months ago by Timothy Allen

5.0 out of 5 stars **Good book**
Good book and a lot of info to take in. Well worth the money I might add.
jay

Published 7 months ago by Jason Anderson

5.0 out of 5 stars **Invaluable information in this great book.**
I bought this book, all I can say is Wow and Thank you! This book is everything and more than what I expected. **Read more**

Published 11 months ago by N. Foy

Making Money

A-Z

with

Self Storage Unit Auctions

2011

Silver Edition

Glendon Cameron

Your Storage Auction Expert

Copyright © 2011 by Glendon Cameron

All rights reserved. No part of this book may be reproduced or transmitted in any form or by any means, electronic or mechanical including photocopying, recording or by any information storage and retrieval system, without written permission in writing from the Publisher.
Conundrum Publishing Company

First Printing 2009 - Making Money A-Z with Self Storage Unit Auctions-

Second Printing 2010- Making Money A-Z with Self Storage Unit Auctions- The Black Edition

This book is dedicated to my grandmother, Mattie Cameron. She taught me to read. If it were not for her love and patience, I have no idea where I would have ended up in this thing called life

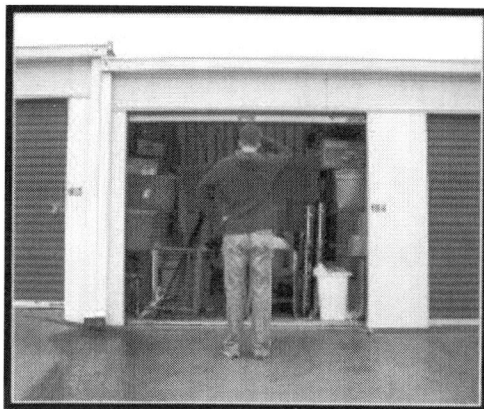

Now that you bought it, what do you do with it?

This book offers a systematic method to finding, buying and selling the items that you get out of storage auction units, at significant profit. Sure, you can start attending storage auctions with no help from me. In some cases you will be successful and more than likely you will make money. Now, the downside is, you will spend money needlessly and on average, it takes a novice three to five years to become really good at. Do you have that much time to be successful? Do you have the money to waste? Would you rather beat your head against the wall when there is a better way?

Of course not! If you want to seriously reduce your learning curve and develop a storage auction business, then you've come to the right place. In many regards, storage auctions are a hidden business. There is nothing, in the way of research on the selling side, which you can get your hands on, other than this book.

There are over 55,000 storage facility companies in the United States of America.

If all of the storage facilities had three auctions per month: 55,000 x 3 =165,000 x 12 that's **1,980,000** storage auction units going up for sale each year!

That is very conservative math. Being inside of the industry, I have known some properties to have as many as 125 storage units at one property going for sale in one month.

There will be some storage facilities which rarely have auctions. Others, you can set your watch by the frequency that they have auctions. This is an educated guess—I believe there are five million plus rooms going for sale across the country, at storage auctions every year. Your major concentration of the auctions will be in urban areas with huge population density. To keep it simple, the more people, the more auctions. If you live in the top 25 high population density areas of the country, you can be assured there will be more auctions in your city than you can attend! This book will help you take maximum advantage of this rich opportunity!

Warning!

You may learn something!

This book is written by a smart-ass in plain English and a conversational tone. Note: there is some cussing and off color jokes included to make things lively. I decided this is the way that I wanted to do it... if you don't like it, man up, you wuss! This way, the ideals and principals described therein flow in an easy–to–follow format and are so simple, a politician could do it!

Disclaimer

This information is designed to provide accurate and authoritative information in regard to the subject matter covered. It is offered with the understanding that the presenters are not engaged in rendering legal, accounting, or other professional services. If legal advice or other expert advice is required, the services of a competent professional should be sought.

Adapted from a Declaration of Principles jointly adopted by a Committee of the American Bar Association and a Committee of Publishers and Associations.

Contents

1

My Beginning

I was presented with an opportunity to make a lot of money very quickly but there was one little problem. It would be unethical as hell to do it! I was an independent contractor for a local contract furniture boutique. If you're sitting in an office right now, contract furniture is the office furniture and cubicles that surround you. It is also retail fixtures and restaurant furniture.

The owner of the company I worked for was a piece of work, to put it lightly, which made my dilemma not that difficult at all because I was looking forward to moving on. I just needed a sign. I had a customer who needed a lot of used office furniture to be liquidated very quickly. Essentially, my contact at this company — who was attempting to sell a great deal of brand new furniture — strongly hinted that whoever could make the used furniture disappear would land the large new furniture contract. None of my secondary market contacts were able to buy the furniture and the clock was ticking!

I had a meeting with the client at 9AM and I needed a solution to this problem, ASAP! On the way to the clients' office, "GC Solutions" was created. In the parking lot, a sketchy business plan was written—in my mind, that is. On the elevator ride up to the 28th floor, I developed the sales pitch and rapid response plan. I walked down the hall still rehearsing what I planned to say and, in the end, got both the new furniture deal and the furniture liquidation deal!

Once the euphoria of what had just happened wore off, a ball of fear started to grow in the pit of my stomach. I had no idea what I was doing or what I was going to do next. My new mindset was formed: "If you're going to screw up, screw up on a grand scale."

Earlier in the year, I recommended to the contract furniture boutique owner that we should try to sell items that had been warehoused for a while on eBay. He shot this suggestion down very quickly! His "no" was quicker than Pookie on crack. In anticipation of a "yes", I had already activated my eBay and PayPal accounts because I thought it was such a great idea. Fortunately for me, he did not think the same.

This was my first experience in selling on eBay and online. After I left my client's office, I immediately went to the job site and began taking pictures. I had over eight floors of office furniture that needed to go quickly. I was there over six hours creating inventory files.

After I got back to my home, I began listing items. It was slow and it took me several hours to do it (this was back in 2001). If only there was the auction management platform back then, well there was I just did not know about it. Listing items on eBay was very labor–intensive and slow. It was a long, long day which did not conclude for me until around twelve that night. I walked in my bedroom and just crashed. I do not even think I took my clothes off.

I got up to a huge surprise the next morning. I had several emails with offers on the furniture. I had priced it too high to give myself some "wiggle" room. At this juncture, I was not really sure how eBay worked (this move was eBay illegal as hell) so I emailed my phone number to the guys who sounded the most serious.

Over the course of the next six weeks, all of the really serious guys came to Atlanta with semi trucks, trailers and crews and moved every stick of the old furniture out of the building. I got a big check for the used furniture and the new office furniture money was coming soon; thus I was introduced to the phenomenal power of eBay!

I started looking for items to sell on my new friend eBay. Since I knew several business owners, I made calls and got deals on unused inventory. For about two years I sold a lot of stuff on eBay in this manner. Ultimately, I had a basement full of non-performing items which were crowding my lifestyle.

Life is what you make it!

I talked my partner into having a garage sale to blow this stuff out! I went online and found a book that gave you tips on how to have a really great and profitable garage sale. It was $9.00 and worth every penny! I was able to move that stuff to the tune of over $1350.00 in two days! I was hooked!

Thus, my introduction to storage unit auctions was launched. I had heard about them, but never went to one. We needed more inventory and this looked like a great avenue to fulfill those requirements. We started off very small in the storage auction business. Being a person that likes to do my research and prepare myself for whatever endeavor is at hand, storage auctions presented a new wrinkle.

It is a cottage industry that is littered with mom and pop type business models. It is very hard to research what appeared to be very close in scope and function to, the black market. There were no books on the subject matter and the references to the business online were a little thin; I knew this was going to be a matter of trial and error. How much error, I was unprepared for. The people that attended the auctions, well many of them, painted a scene from the movie "Deliverance."

This created a certain level of cockiness in me, which did not serve me well. Other than attending a few auctions before I bought anything, I broke every rule in the book. I bought the wrong stuff, pissed off the wrong people and was put through a quasi-initiation ritual.

The deal on the storage auction trail is, newbies are a pain in the ass. I was a newbie, therefore I was automatically wrong. In spite of all of this bad judgment and harassment, I still made money from day one. If I had a comprehensive book on storage auctions, such as the one you are reading, there is no telling how much money I could've made back then.

Once I learned the lay of the land, the business progressed at a very fast clip, into a thriving resale business. I am going to outline for you the steps I took to start and grow that business. It is a business based on the misfortune of others; however, that is life in the good old United States of America. If you do not pay your bills, they will take your stuff. That is another thing that you can count on in life, like death and taxes.

If you are the very sentimental type, this business may not be for you. If not, read on. There is loads of information in this book that will help you be successful and make money. Most people have no idea how much money you can make doing this and that is the beauty of the business. It changed my life, maybe it will change yours!

Why Are There So Many Auctions?

A question that I often receive is "why would someone lose such valuable things? In your videos on YouTube, you talk about and actually show some very nice stuff that you got out of storage auction units! How in the hell would someone let that go?"

This is a valid question. During my first few months in the business, I asked the same question over and over. It did not make sense to me that someone would allow fabulous and grand personal belongings to be sold in a lien sale (the legal name for a storage auction sale).

Some of the reasons make a great deal of sense. Other reasons and situations can be mind boggling! The number one reason that people lose their possessions at a storage auction sale is the lack of money. They're totally tapped out, that makes a lot of sense.

The next common reasons also make perfectly good sense, death and incarceration. Often people pass on or they may become ill and spend an extended period of time in the hospital.

When you sign your storage unit papers, there's a section for alternate contact information, next of kin and secondary contact information in case something does happen to the renter. There are quite a few folks which leave that section blank and or put down fictitious information, because they do not want anyone in their business.

I have been in the storage facility office when a property manager was making phone calls to find out why the tenant was no longer paying. Wrong numbers, I never heard of that person and addresses that do not exist, were common! Storage facilities extend great effort in determining what is happening with a tenant and to ensure they do not lose their possessions, if at all possible.

"When someone goes to jail, there is usually a good reason for them going to jail. If that person is unable to bond out and make bail, the chances are very good that they will not have the money to pay their storage unit bill. Also, because they are incarcerated, many of their friends and family members will be reluctant to extend a loan or pay their bills.

One of the best units I have ever seen went to auction because of this very reason. The gentleman lost many high grade antiques because he had no one to help him out with his unit. The storage facility knew exactly where he was. They tried to help him. They held off selling his unit for seven months! It still went to auction, even with that courtesy extended. When it became abundantly clear he was not getting out of jail that year, they sold his unit."

Now for the unique and strange!

I bought a unit that went up for auction, not because the owner was broke or in jail. He just did not give a damn. This person decided to leave the United States and move to Japan to pursue his passion of martial arts training and establish a Do Jo. He called up to the storage facility and said "I no longer care about such things, do what you want with it" and hung up the phone. They called him repeatedly, he never responded, thus they sold his stuff to me! It was a damn good unit!

Atlanta is a very transient city. There are roughly 10,000 people a month moving into the metro Atlanta area. On average, 4000 people a month *leave* the metropolitan area. Some of these folks do not plan well. They put all their possessions in a storage unit and move to say, California. After a few weeks or months it becomes financially infeasible to come back and pick up their items, so they just let the unit go.

If you are moving cross-country, do not put your stuff in a storage facility!!!!

It is a waste of money and you would be better served by taking what you can with you and selling what you can't take with you. This is why, after a long period of time, you forget what is in that unit and eventually replace everything that you already have. This creates a strange situation. You have this unit that you're paying a lot of money on, but you do not need any of the items in that unit. Just sell the stuff folks, sell it! I understand you are saying shut the hell up Glendon! But trust me I have seen this situation a thousand times!

Another situation is divorce which can lead to a lack of money or, in this case, madness! There was a couple that was getting a divorce. They hated each other! They had a unit full of household items that they shared. Because they hated each other, they could never work out the time to clean out the unit. It became so bad, that they both stopped paying the rent. If you've ever seen a marriage dissolve in divorce, you know many nutty situations can occur. This feuding couple must have forgotten about the Yamaha grand piano and the several paintings of well known local artists that were in the unit.

One of the saddest reasons I know that many people lose their storage unit, is alcohol and drug addiction. There are often signs of the problem in the unit. You would be amazed at some of the well known people that have lost their possessions in a storage auction in Atlanta for this reason.

This is somewhat crazy; many people lose their units because of "inertia." These people have the money to pay the rent; the problem is they are just sick and tired of the stuff and let it go. It happens quite a bit and I know many of the back stories of people whose unit I bought at a storage auction. Sometimes when you buy the unit it is very easy to figure out why they lost it.

There are some people that feel it is not right for the storage facility to sell the property of delinquent tenants. What many of those people fail to realize is, the vast majority of people that lose their storage units at auction, do so for some dumb ass reasons. Bad things happen to good people all of the time.

It is one thing to be hit by a truck while you are crossing the street and end up in the hospital creating a situation that causes you to lose your stuff. It is an animal of an entirely different complexion when you lose your stuff because you're sniffing cocaine every day and lose your $280,000 a year job! Call me heartless, but the person doing drugs, getting drunk and making some piss poor lifestyle decisions will gather no sympathy from me. When you gather a little steam and start building your business, you will see what I mean. It only takes a few weeks or months to understand why so many people lose their personal possessions at a storage unit auction.

2

A Hidden Marketplace

In the United States, at some point, most of the self storage facilities will have an auction or sale to vacate non–paying tenants according to the laws in their particular state. There are no formal numbers on the number of sales; however, I can tell you every major city and its' suburbs are going to have thousands of these storage auction unit sales every year!

These auctions are open to the public and they do not require that you have any special permits to buy, with one exception: if you have a business, you will save money by presenting your resale certificate. This enables you to buy items and not pay sales tax on the item. Some auctions charge sales tax and some do not. Ask when you call to inquire about the auction whether or not they charge sales tax.

Think about how many of these storage facilities that you have passed going to work, in your travels and in your backyard! You are literally driving by money, every day! More storage properties are being built every day because it is one of the best ROI real estate investments one can make. Most business owners that invest in storage properties usually recoup original investment after three years. From that point forward it is a cash cow!

I want to clear up some confusion. There are many books online about storage auctions and the storage business, and these are entirely two different things! If you are buying additional books about storage auctions, really read the information on the back and front of the book. A storage business is actually investing in or building the storage facilities. Making money with storage auctions is buying the contents of storage units when the owners do not pay. I am not trying to be either simple or offensive but over the last year, I have noticed many people buying my book and the storage business books together! We're talking about two completely different animals and if you do not have $50,000 up to a few 1,000,000 dollars just lying around, it is something to think about. Back to making money with storage auctions!

For people selling online at eBay and Craigslist, you can get a ton for your merchandise at these auctions. Most flea market sellers know about these auctions and find it to be a resource for items to resale. Many flea market vendors do not even get in the auctions. They wait until newly minted storage auction buyers come to the flea market. When you're a newbie in the business, sometimes the need to recoup your capital exceeds your good judgment. Many of these veteran flea market vendors will fleece the hell out of you! Please take a moment and think about it; they are coming to you (if you are that guy) to buy your merchandise and resell it in the same marketplace that you're setting up your wares to sell. It does not take a rocket scientist to know that something's amiss!

In the early days of this business, (and I always treated it as a business although for many it is a hobby), storage facilities *gave* the items out of the storage units away! There were not a lot of people interested in the items and the storage companies had to beg people to take the stuff or they paid someone to trash it! Can you imagine thousands of dollars of merchandise free of charge only requiring sweat equity!

Yes, things have changed tremendously. In earlier years I have seen units go for a dollar or as high as fifteen! It all depends on what you see at the door. For many years this was a secret source of inventory for antique stores, thrift stores, flea market vendors, used furniture stores and the perpetually curious. It was and still is a very insular community. Unless you are a regular, no one really talks to you and they may bid higher than normal to run you off!

Life is what you make it!

Some storage auction folk are very territorial; they will lose money to ensure that you do not make any money! Yes, it sounds crazy but this is the way they do it.

If you weathered the storm and managed to make it through the initiation of becoming a storage auction buyer, sooner or later you will hit a big score. My first big score earned me more money in a few months than most of the people in our country make in a year! It can be frustrating to watch a newcomer buy a unit and make out like a fat rat, while you have not gotten anything decent in weeks or months.

Things remained like this for years then over time, more and more people got into the business. The prices have increased but you can still snag a great deal or several, a month, if you know what you are doing. Don't be fooled by the sometimes homeless and ragged appearance of the regulars. They are a crafty lot and many of them are quite well off; some are even rich. Sometimes all it takes is one unit to change your life! I bought twenty that I will never forget! I will go into detail about those buys later on. I will say this, if you are not afraid of hard work and can follow simple directions, you can make a decent income following the business plan I developed in the course of my business. If you are a real go getter, you can make a six figure income. I did and so can you.

Storage unit auctions are part of the legal proceeding that storage unit companies utilize to reclaim the storage unit space to rent to a paying customer. The legal actions are essentially the same as a tenant eviction process. There will be different nuisances to the law, depending upon which jurisdiction the storage facility falls in. I am in the metro Atlanta area where, on any given month, 1,500–2,500 rooms or more go up for auction. I can imagine in a city like New York it would be much greater. To be delinquent after 60–90 days of nonpayment the storage facility, after filing a dispossession writ, can legally sell the contents of the storage unit to reclaim their space. Sometimes it can be done in sixty days.

Right up until the auctioneer or manager for the storage facility says "sold", the contents of the unit still belongs to the renter. Hence, the no touching or sorting through the unit until it is sold rule. This rule is not always followed. If there is a large crowd and the managers do not keep people from the door, people will go through whatever they can get their paws on!

This usually increases the bidding if someone sees something valuable—not always a good thing. In the case that it is absolute junk, it can save you money. I prefer to stand from the door and bid on what I see. You get better deals when other bidders cannot see what is in the unit.

There is definitely an art to bidding and some science to bidding. For a person who knows a little about everything, this is a great opportunity for you. Knowledge has always been and always will be what separates the successful from the unsuccessful in all walks of life. This is vitally important in this business. This is an exciting and at the same time tragic business. You are making money off of the loss of someone else.

Philosophically, some people have a problem with this and you will hear and see things that will tug on your heart strings, so this business is not for the faint of heart. If you are not put off by this, get ready for the ride of your life. There is an awesome reward waiting on those who apply the lessons of this book whole heartedly. You are going to have to work your ass off, but it will be worth it! You will see things and learn about things you never thought about!

Over the years, I have learned so much about culture, people, human nature and things I had no clue existed in the world by the things I find in storage unit auctions. I have furnished my house, gotten a new wardrobe, high-end electronics, high-end watches, guns and more out of storage units. Sometimes you just cannot believe what people leave in the rooms. Understand, these people never expected to lose their stuff —that's why it is in the unit! I have gotten everything from gold to guns out of storage units. There is no telling what you may find!

Being a professional storage auction buyer or even a part-time storage auction buyer is full of hidden advantages. Right now, there are many items in your home that you do not even think about, until you run out of that particular item. Toilet paper, soap, dishwashing detergent, washing powder, toothpaste, car wash, and even alcoholic beverages, such as rum and vodka, are all items I have obtained from a storage auction unit. Hold on, I know none of this sounds very exciting, well maybe the alcohol does.

This is the exciting aspect of finding regularly needed items in a storage auction unit. You no longer have to buy the item out of the store. To give you a great example; I recently ran out of toilet paper that I got out of a unit two years ago. The unit cost me $350; I made well over $1000 and I kept the palette of toilet paper that was in the unit. For two years and some months I have not had to pay for toilet paper for my home. Here's a quick calculation: since I am now back in the marketplace for toilet paper, the stuff that I like costs roughly $10.00 a month. I saved over $300 on that one household expenditure alone!

There are many other things that I did not have to buy for my house. Cement, paint, weather stripping—these are things that can cost a lot of money so getting them out of the storage unit saved me a tremendous amount of money over the years. Currently, I am experiencing sticker shock over clothing and other items. When you're used to getting everything at an awesome discount, it changes you. This is the life of a storage auction buyer. You can make money coming and going. For a thrifty person, this is the business to be a part of.

Now that I think of it, I'm about to run out of cologne. It is odd. I've had every type of cologne in the world and I have not paid for it directly in the last seven years. It's pretty amazing when you think about it.

Life is what you make it!

3

Time to Jump In!

Having the Right Mind-Set

One of the most important aspects of the storage auction business is the mental aspect. When I first entered the storage auction business, I was full of enthusiasm and optimism. If you are the type of person that thinks the world is out to get you, you may not want to get in this business. Being a storage auction buyer requires a lot of faith... faith in self, your own ability and your sense of judgment.

If you are flaky and cannot commit to anything for more than a few weeks or months, you're not going to go far in life, this business or in any other event. There will be highs and lows in this business—frequently and in the same day. I want you to be successful. One key that unlocks the door to being successful is to become what you think about. A positive mindset, (not a Polly Anna all is well in the world mindset) means that in spite of adversity, you will win.

When you think about winning and there's no action behind the thought process, you will not do well. If you are working your ass off and you constantly ask yourself "what is the point ... I am just going to fail no matter how hard I try," you're setting yourself up to fail! You're putting forth the effort physically and kicking your own ass mentally. You will be frustrated and despondent. When you marry a great mind-set with a tremendous work ethic, this is when you get the Michael Jordan's and Bill Gates of the world.

A belief in self and high level of personal self-efficacy, are requirements to being successful. These elements are so critical to success that a person in possession of both can beat and surpass people who are smarter, faster and naturally gifted, but lazy. I am not the smartest person in the world, not even close to it, but I will work harder and outperform most individuals. It is these traits that allowed me to beat people who had more capital than I did in the storage auction business. The good news is these are attributes that anyone can develop. It is a matter of practice and a burning devotion to your inner self, to be better the next day than the day before.

To really drive this point home, I have a speech impediment and I am mildly dyslexic. The very things that I was naturally deficient and personally challenged in performing each and every day such as reading, writing and speaking, I now do for a living. When I say that this stuff is important, I am speaking from personal experience.

Get Your Work Out On!

I will be clear; unless you've had some type of manual labor job, say like loading bricks, this will be the hardest occupation that you have ever under taken. I suggest undertaking a fitness program, if you are currently not working out. Working out not only improves your physical fitness for this business, it will clear your mind and you will sleep better at night. I recommend a component of weight training, since you will be moving stuff as a cornerstone of your workout regimen. It also helps with the mental components of being an entrepreneur. That is correct; by initiating this business startup, that is exactly what you are.

Have a Plan

The first thing you will need is a business plan. Many people in this business buy first and hope to make money later. You really do not want to be one of those people. I have heard so many times, **"I hope to make this or I should at least get my money back."** People making those types of statements do not have a plan to build and grow their businesses. Many will pretty much spin their wheels—it is an awful thing to go nowhere fast! I know of folks who have been in this business almost as long as I have been alive and they do not do well consistently. They are just addicted to the high of new auctions. Everyone I know that is in the business and has been an auction hound for more than a few years has had a **"BIG HIT."** That is a nice add-on, but the key to making it in this business is making money on the regular basis, preferably weekly. This is where the planning comes into play. There are certain components of this business that will make that possible.

By having a system, you will, to some degree of predictable accuracy, forecast your sales from the beginning. Month after month they should go up, because you should be going from no sales to some sales. Another way that you will consistently make money is "**build up.**" When you buy a unit, you do not always sell everything fast, which is a good thing—if you got it cheap enough. Part of making money consistently is you will get hot stuff that will sale very quickly.

Most auction hounds want to blow it out, get paid and buy again. There are two problems with this method of running your business. You sell some items far too cheaply and you will kill yourself, working that hard. Unless they get very lucky with a huge buy and it does happen, it has happened to me. As I said before large jackpot units are the icing on the cake, not the cake itself. There is a much better way!

However, can you build a business on luck? I did not think so either! That is not the name of the game! You want to make money in an orderly and predictable manner to the best of your abilities. As we go forward, I will show you how to do just that! With hard work, planning and a good work ethic, you can make great money and enjoy yourself! The money you can make will be based on your resources:

- Capital
- Time
- A place to sell, and
- Labor

Once you buy a room, you can get a feel on how to proceed in making income with a storage units' inventory.

By having a solid business plan you can get to the top of the heap rather quickly. Think in terms of a marathon, not a sprint—base hits versus home runs. This mindset will carry you far in this business. If you have never done anything in your life like this, you should know all good things in life take time, in most cases.

Know in the beginning you will make mistakes. We all did and this will happen. For me, this was like going to Las Vegas and winning 90% of the time, with 10% being losers. To me, those are stunning odds! If it is just you entering in this business and you don't think you can gather any assistance on the clean outs, then my friend, you have two choices:

1) Outsource your labor, or

2) Buy only units with loads that you can personally handle; which will limit your time and income to a degree. You can expand as your sales grow.

You can get awesome deals out of any size room; however, the more you buy, the luckier you become. If you are doing it all (I did for awhile) you will come up short in a couple of areas: Your energy level for one and your personal life on the other hand.

Life is what you make it!

The breakdown for your storage auctions business process is-->

Going to auctions—this can be a very time consuming part of your process. Auctions are usually held Monday–Friday during normal business hours.

Loading—proper loading techniques are very important. There is a procedure to loading a truck. You want to ensure that your new merchandise makes it your warehouse intact.

Sorting—unless the unit is one item or a large item, sorting becomes a crucial part of your business. It is best to put aside the items that you're certain of the selling price. Take your time with the next step.

Item lookups—when you are just beginning, you will not have a large knowledge base of stuff, this will be a very large percentage of time spent on your business. You do want to take the time and look up any item that you're uncertain of the price and you want to **check at least three different sources.** That will give you an idea of the average fair market price. If you have a situation where it is difficult to find the price of the item, then you will need the help of an outside source ... an expert. More often than not, when you cannot find a price of the item online through your research, it's usually not worth that much.

Pricing—price your items to sell. At the time of this writing, we are experiencing dire economic circumstances. We're living in times that are dominated by downward pricing pressure. Homes that once sold for $300,000 are now selling for half of that and in some really distressed markets, even less! After doing your research, price all of your items with what I refer to as "wiggle room." There are a few instances where you can raise the price of an item. In the other 95% of the time, you should position yourself with room for negotiation.

Here is an example of pricing: a used washer and dryer sets sell from $100 to $750. There are many variables that come into play in selling the used washer and dryer set such as the name brand, special features, age and condition. If, in your possession, is a mid-range washer and dryer set, you determine that you can sell that washer and dryer set at a price point between $250 & $325. After noting the price of the washer and dryers currently in the marketplace, you deduce that the most that you can get for your set is $280. When a customer calls you, you're prepared. When placing your item in the marketplace, you will price the item at the top end of the price point. You know if you get more than $280 for the set that adds sweetener on the deal. In the case of someone offering you $275, you will take it! It will be stupid to leave $275 on the table holding out for an additional $5.00! I see this happen all of the time.

Listing items online—we will go much deeper into this in a later chapter. Listing your items for sale online, will be a huge part of your success. If you live in a small town and you are the only resale merchant in your neck of the woods, you can charge what you want—you have no competition. This is a very rare position to be in.

Selling—you will spend a third of your time selling or answering sales related questions. The exceptions to this rule will be if you have a sales organization with a full time salesperson.

Repairs—repairs are a necessary evil. Often when people move their possessions without the assistance of a professional mover, many bad things happen, such as scratched and broken items, and missing parts. A great majority of the time, many items can be repaired or restored to a sellable condition. If you want to conduct repairs, you should know it is very time consuming and you will need space to fix the items. Often, repairs can be the difference between realizing an OK profit to a significant profit.

As you can see, there are many steps to becoming a successful storage auction buyer. Each of those steps is just as important as the preceding step. Imagine if you will, your business is a huge jigsaw puzzle and for it to look like the great portrait that it is, all pieces most fit in their proper place. Otherwise, the visual integrity of the puzzle is jacked! There are only so many hours in a day. You want to be efficient as possible with time and resources. After you take stock of your resources, then you will know what types of units you can buy.

I highly recommend getting to the point of buying bigger units or a lot of units as soon as possible. I've said it once I've said it before—the more you buy the luckier you will become. I am not one to blow smoke up your ass, this book will be straightforward and to the point. Your time is valuable. Sure you will get a 5x5 or 5X10 loaded with valuable stuff, but I have found the best stuff consistently in the larger units 10X10, 10X15, 10X20, 10X30, 10X40 and larger!   This is the reason why: anything in your house or place of business can be in a storage unit. If you buy a large one, there is no telling what is in the back of the unit. This is part of the fun!

I have gone to clean out units and I get to the back and there is a front loader washer and dryer set, huge air compressors and pallets of equipment (that was a bitch to move), forklift stuff I cannot move by myself. After two years into the business, we hired a load crew. There is no way you can buy twenty five to forty storage units a month, clean, process and sell all of the contents of the units by yourself. It can be exhausting! On and off I would hire people for the bigger units, but I loaded most of the smaller ones myself and I have the muscles to prove it!

The larger income comes from scale and volume. The same principles apply even if you want to do it part time. Before you go any further, I want you to stop and write down your goals— personal development, income and life goals. It is really hard to get someplace if you do not know where you are going! Don't worry; there are no wrong answers in this exercise. Uncovering what you want out of life is the most important thing. I am very serious about this exercise. I grew up really poor, coming from impoverished beginnings! Learning how to set goals and accomplish goals, improved my confidence and life. With goals, effort and planning you can go very far in life!

☒ PERSONAL GOALS:

_____

_____

Life is what you make it!

_____
_____
_____
_____
_____
_____
_____
_____
_____
_____
_____
_____
_____
_____
_____
_____
_____

INCOME GOALS:

_____
_____
_____
_____
_____
_____
_____
_____
_____
_____

Life is what you make it!

_____
_____
_____
_____
_____
_____
_____
_____
_____
_____

☒ LIFE GOALS:

_____
_____
_____
_____
_____
_____
_____
_____
_____
_____
_____
_____
_____
_____
_____
_____
_____
_____

Life is what you make it!

I know if you've never thought about this, it can be a somewhat challenging task; nevertheless, it is worth the effort. I will give you some examples on how to proceed.

I want to earn $_____ per month with my part time business.

I want to restructure my 401K and I will need $_____ per month to do this.

I want a way for my wife to earn extra money and still stay at home with the kids.

I am retired and I want to supplement my fixed income by $_____ per month

Those are just a little food for thought. I find that writing down your goals makes the whims of your mind into something real and tangible. After you have written your goals, the next step is the plan of execution ... how, when, and where you are going to start this business and make money. Remember to think of it as a business first and foremost. By writing down every step, you will be well ahead of the competition that doesn't plan.

Business plans do not have to be complex. It can be as simple as this.

Capital = $500.00   Sales Goal = $2000.00 per month

I will only buy units in the price range of $25–$90.00 and sell the items that are not suitable for **ebay/Amazon** on Craigslist, if at all possible. If the item is not suitable for online sale, I will sell it at a garage sale, donate the items to charity or throw those items away. After I start making sales, a certain percentage will be reinvested back into the business. Once I reach my operating budget target, I will reassess and make a new goal for a larger budget, based on the sales I have and how long it took me to reach my first targeted budget.

(My recommendation is put all money earned from sales back in the business to quickly reach $2,500-$3,000 in operating capital.)

Yes it can be just that simple! When I speak of a business plan, it is not a twenty page thesis. It is just a written guideline on how to run your business. When what you are doing can be measured and quantified it can be improved. Without keeping track of these metrics, you have no idea how well or how poorly you are doing in regards to profit and loss.

I do understand that everyone will not be able to reinvest 100% back into their business initially. For some of you, it will take a few months or years, if you're starting with absolutely nothing, in terms of operating capital. As an old neighbor of mine would often say, *"if you live long enough, you will get old!"* Whether you're actively planning for your future or not, the time will still pass. You might as well address the needs of your future with a solid plan.

We live in a microwave society in need of immediate gratification. It is my opinion that this mindset leads to more failures and disappointments than any other reason in our society. We have become seduced by the concept of **"the overnight success story."** Most businesses take 2–5 years to begin generating a healthy profit. This is normal and the reasons are many. When you start a new business you do not know what the hell you are doing, markets change, leadership may be poor, etc. The beauty of the storage auction business is, with the proper guidance, you can be earning a significant income within six months to one year. Regardless of the fact that you may have the best business plan in the world, there are many contingencies that you cannot plan for. This is not to say do not develop a business plan—this is to say do not write a business plan in stone because conditions will change and your plan will need revising whether the business is doing well or poorly.

I'm just giving you the knowledge you will need. **This will be an ongoing process; your ultimate goal is to arrive at the operating budget of $10,000–$15,000.** At this level, you will be in the **top 5% of your storage auction competition.** Most people stall out at an operating budget of $3000. With this operating budget, you aren't positioned to buy week after week. With an operating budget of $10,000-$15,000 you will be in great shape!

Regardless of the fact that your sales channels may be slow, don't panic—it is part of the business. In a retail environment, this will be the case on occasion and during certain seasons. In my eight years of selling the contents of storage auctions, the summer is always slow compared to the time period of fall through spring.

The beauty of what many see to be a problem is actually a grand opportunity.

If your sales are slow, chances are, your competitors will also be slow. This means they will not be in a financial position to take advantage of the opportunities that will arise during this slow period. The deals never stop, they just become sweeter. I took note of this fact one summer. Units that would cost $1200, $1500 or even $3000 during the fall were consistently selling for 40%-60% less during the summer. With such a huge differential in unit costs for the same type of merchandise, it made sense to buy and hold until the fall, which is something that I started to do that year. This one change in my business practice totally invigorated my business and almost tripled my revenue.

You may become very lucky and buy a unit that gives you this type of operating capital; I just want you to be smart about this and to do well. Your operating capital will be the lever to move your business forward. Let me break this down for you...

It is not just about having the capital to buy, you want to create consistent cash flow to maintain this level of operating capital.

You want to be in the position to always have money to buy storage auction units. There are many people that will buy a storage auction unit, with the plan to sell the contents of that unit before they buy another storage auction unit. This plan sounds good on the surface, but it is problematic for several reasons. Following this method when you have the cash to buy, will lead to lost opportunities. These are some examples of what I am talking about.

Action Sheet   02/13/03   -   03/13/03

Budget 1500.00
I will buy units in the price range of $25–$500.00 dollars, seeking two 10 x 20s this month!
Funds for Inventory 1250.00

Truck Rental 150.00

Fuel 50.00

Incidentals 50.00

Goal 6000.00 in salesCosts/Actual Results

Truck 285.00

Fuel 135.00

425.00 Unit 1030   made 1850.00

325.00 Unit 221   made 720.00

385.00 Unit 2006   lost 200 broke even 185.00

95.00   Unit 186   made 2600.00

5.00   Unit 876   made 400.00

Total 5755-1740=4015 profit

This was great. I was just a little short of plan but within a year, I was generating these figures per week! I know of no other business that you can make such a dramatic leap of income, without having a massive cash infusion, which was not the case in my business!

A. **It is a Monday**, you have just bought three storage auction units, and you still have money left over in your operating budget. However, you decide not to go out again until all of the contents of the storage of the units that you just bought are sold. Why is this problematic? Today is Monday and there are auctions every day for the rest of the week. It is true that you may not find anything better than what you currently bought. What is also a possibility is that you will buy one unit during the rest of the week, which will pay for all of the units that you have bought for the month. The more that you buy, the luckier you become.

B. **You have almost sold** everything from your previous storage auction buy. You have money, but you're not going out again until you sell everything. This is a very bad strategy. You lose a great deal of time following this method. You will have been better off attending all of the auctions that you could have attended during that time frame. Storage auctions are strange beasts. One week could be utter garbage. The next week you will want to buy every unit that you see.

Another lost opportunity is there are numbers of people who are operating on the same paradigm concept that you are. Which means, by the luck of the draw, you will attend auctions that do not have that many attendees; thus, you will be in the position to buy great merchandise at an even greater discount! There's an old merchandising axiom **"you make your money**

when you buy your inventory, not when you sell it." The reason for this is very simple. When you buy your inventory, that price never changes. The price that you initially put on your items to sell has a very good chance of changing and not always in a positive direction. This is why you want to get your items to resale at a serious discount and storage auction units give you this ability —in a manner that will be very hard for another business model to replicate. You truly are buying your stock for pennies on the dollar.

C. **You are in possession of merchandise that I call," lame duck stock"** you have lowered the price and advertised it over in over and it is not moving. You have vowed that you will not buy another storage auction unit until you sell this stuff. In the meantime, better merchandise is being bought by other people. Sometimes you will buy dead stock... sell it really cheap or donate it and move on. I know of one storage auction buyer that held on to his stuff for six months until he sold it all! During that six month timeframe, I came across five jackpot units. You cannot win the game if you do not suit up!

I think it should be clear to you by now; your storage auction business is one of fluctuation. As long as your cash flow is consistent you will be fine. The problems crop up when you go weeks without a sale. If you're working from home, that means your storage space is held hostage, that's why it is so important to keep abreast of the metrics of your business. Numbers never lie; you may not like what they're saying at that moment but the numbers always speak the truth.

I have spoken to many auction hounds and they "**kinda, sorta"** know where they are financially, meaning they know if they made money or lost money. They have no clue as to how much or how little they are really making. Without the hard costs of fuel, rent, repairs on the budget sheet, you could be losing money and not even know it! This takes analysis and when you get this down pat, it saves you time and money.

After trending our business for a few months, I noticed we consistently did better financially with the larger units, only lost on one out of ninety five large units in a four month period! With this information, I began to buy larger units or full units. It was hard to maintain this discipline!

I would see smaller units—they were good, really good— but I knew since most people would bid on them, the cost-to- profit ratio was going to be skewed unfavorably for our business.

I saw this over and over, smaller units going proportionally higher than the larger units.

Why?

Simple, most people can handle the smaller units, where only about 20% of the folks coming out to the auction could handle the larger units. You need help, a big truck and space to store all of that stuff. I remember one auction in particular where this was so pronounced. I bought a hallway unit, which was a 10 X 20 jammed packed for $520.00 and a smaller unit which was very clean and had some unusual looking stuff in it, went for $430.00, to another buyer—he got half of what I bought with only a $90.00 differential in price! It was shocking; during the auction, with the adrenaline pumping, most people are not paying attention to trends. I was in on it up until $230 and I let it go, good thing too, the boxes in the back were empty! I saw this happen over and over.

I am not a genius; I learned this information because I took time to note bidder behavior. Believe it or not a lot of people place bids based on ability to haul, so the smaller units can be more expensive proportionally. I noticed it for a while, before the dots connected, but when it hit home it was like thunder!

(For the people I spoke to who bought the first version of this book, it's not as competitive in other areas.)

You may be in luck; it all depends on where you live in the country. I highly recommend going out to the auctions for a few weeks before you buy, with a pen and paper and take note of what you see (this will freak out the regulars). Watch who bids and who gets respect. It will be a tremendous advantage to you to know the lay of the land before you start bidding and buying. There are some people you cannot outbid. All you are going to do is frustrate yourself and piss them off. You can outsmart them—there will always be people losing their units, you can count on that.

Life is what you make it!

We started this business up after a tremendous garage sale. I bought this book online about how to have a garage sale. This manual really helped us grow in ways I never thought possible. To address the needs of storage auction buyers, I wrote *"The Ultimate Garage Sale."* You can buy it from me at www.urbanpackrat.com or purchase it online.

If you do not have any money to get started, this is a great way to raise money for your new venture without impacting your paycheck or savings account.   Just go around your home and find items that you do not need or can part with and have a sale. People love garage sales more than I can say! That is what got me hooked! This is also a great way to start practicing how you are going to deal with the public.   Even in the resale business, customer service will make you or break you. If you never sold anything, I suggest reading books on sales and marketing, then apply what you have learned to your particular market and sales strategy. Different parts of the country are going to require you to get deep into your market. In a word, you are going to have to test the waters and see what works for your business. It is part of the fun!

Some of you will be in the cat bird seat as far as auctions are concerned.   I talked to one guy who says he has no competition in his part of the country. That is a lovely position to be in as a storage auction buyer!

To some it looks like junk, but to the well trained eye, this is money! Check out how neat this unit is! That wire rack is $50.00 by itself! This is a good unit! I want you to create a template that will keep you heading in the right direction. I will give you my first business plan, how I developed it. See the chart on the next page.

As you can see, I went over my budget by the tune of two hundred and forty dollars. This is the rub, if I did not have a budget I would have not known that I even went over budget! This is a salient point; you must know where you're starting in order to know when you've arrived at your destination on time. Anything can happen when you do not have a budget. You can be leaking money and not even be aware of it, until it is too late! You need to know the condition of your money at all times!

Does this make sense to you?

Metrics are a key component to this business; you have to watch your sales and cash flow like a hawk! I have seen many people spend every dollar in their pocket to win a unit at auction. Unless that unit is a killer unit, the outcome is usually bad—really bad. This happens because the person bidding became **"caught up"** in the action.

I have witnessed many very good units sold for too much money. It does not matter how good the unit may be, you won't realize a profit if you spend more money buying it than you can make on the re-sales. Your number one goal is preservation of capital—preserving capital and having that capital make money for you. The storage auction business brings out a certain personality type, one that is prone to gambling. I will not say that you will never get caught up; with the esoteric nature of storage auctions you can spend more than you intended and still come out very well on your balance sheet, based on what is in the storage unit.

You are already broke and the unit you just bought may put you in the red. Be smart and have a game plan. Don't be like the large number of people in the storage unit business who do not make a profit, who generate very little revenue, or very slim profit margins at best. **This is called turning money where the whole focus is buying to buy and hope to make money.** No good can come from this method. It is a business plan, (I use the term loosely) predicated on luck. It is this gamblers mindset that creates those pitiful margins. Some of these folks spend thousands of dollars per month with little return. Of course they make some money and occasionally they hit big. This is what fuels the addiction of racing from one storage unit to another to get that buying high. The closest thing I can think of, in parallel, is a crack-head on the pipe. You will know these folks by their jumpy posture. Once the bidding begins; you can see it in their beady little eyes.

Be cool and detached, think about what you are doing and always keep your goals for the business foremost in your mind. After you have sat down and worked out your goals and written up your budget, you now have the framework for your business plan. Your plan will become clearer and more defined as you start buying and selling. The evolution of your business plan will be ongoing as you gain experience and more capital. You will revise it to grow or maintain your business as you grow and learn more about selling and making money in your part of the country.

The same applies to your goal sheet, which I recommend that you look over daily to keep your objectives fresh in your mind. The setting of goals and writing those goals down creates a framework that will give you a clear view of what you want this business to do for you. Many people that I have spoken to, often tell me they have their goals in their mind and that method works well for their goal setting resolutions. I will not doubt their sincerity but what I know to be true is a written goal works wonders for your future. By writing down your goals, you will achieve those goals much quicker, because the act of writing down your goals gives you a process to follow. When you approach an endeavor, or task with no clear plan on how to engage that task, the time to complete the task usually takes much longer than if you have a clear cut plan of attack.

If you change your mind about certain goals, no problem, just put the new goal on the sheet and work out a plan to achieve it! None of this stuff is set in stone. Think of your goals and business plan as a map that will get you to your destination. With any journey, there are unexpected obstacles and detours we must tackle; having a plan will help you overcome these situations much easier than having no plan at all. If this sounds like a broken record, it is, and more than likely you will see these words **plan, goals and business plan, again and again.** I am one that likes to fly by the seat of my pants which does work... sometimes; however, you will discover just like I did you will be more effective and focused with a plan of action. One that is written down and revised on occasion to deal with the events life throws at us. The other stuff is simple! Once you have figured out why you want to do this, you will have much more motivation which is essential to your success. Trust me; it will be about more than the money.

Life is what you make it!

Sometime being successful is reason enough to do the thing!

4

The Tools You Need To Be Successful

Issues to be solved before you buy your first unit.

New folks do not get a lot of respect because they really do not know what's going on. Storage auctions, or lien sales, are a very sensitive aspect in the storage business. There are so many things that can go wrong and blow up in the face of the storage facility owner that it is no wonder that they are a little cautious with the proceedings of evicting the contents of a delinquent tenant off of their property.

Even though the intent of the storage business owner is to vacate the delinquent unit and rent it to a paying customer, many storage businesses will bend over backwards to accommodate delinquent tenants. Some of the things that I have seen and overheard include taking half of the delinquent amount and the tenant vacates the unit immediately. Sometimes, the storage facility will take even less than half. Most storage facilities lose money on 90% of the auctions they have! The storage business is a very lucrative business. The owners of the storage properties do not need to sell the stuff of tenants to make money. Many of the owners are already very well off to downright rich.

I want to paint a better picture for you which will prepare you for some of the difficulties that you will encounter while prepping for your first few auctions. It is not personal, but at times it sure feels like it.

Before you can jump in, you need to know where the water is.

There are many things that should be done before you buy your first storage auction unit. To many, this list will seem like overkill. In my opinion, I find it best to be prepared for any situation. Due to the unpredictable nature of a storage auction unit, it is best to have the tools of the trade in your car or truck (more on those items going forward). The most critical element to being successful with storage auctions as a business is knowledge. Having access to and applying the knowledge that others in the business thought was not important, was the reason I was able to do so well, so quickly, in the storage auction business.

You need to know when and where **ALL** of the auctions are happening in your area. Check the legal section of your local newspaper or just call up the storage facility directly to inquire when the next auction is happening. **Calling is the best option** and it is wise to create your own schedule on a spreadsheet. Also, program the numbers in your mobile phone as you call the storage facilities—this is a tremendous time saver as you will be calling these businesses again and again. The process of calling storage businesses will be easy in some cases and frustrating as hell in others.

Many will not call you back. Some will tell you that they do not ever have auctions, and later on you will see that they *are* having auctions. It is a great idea to constantly and consistently check back with these locations because storage facilities are often bought and sold like stocks. New management will always have new policies. Speaking of new management, whenever you see a new storage business being built or recently opened, stop by to introduce yourself and make it a point to call them every month. Typically, it takes a new property six months to one year before they will start having auctions. If it is a brand new storage business owner that is not well versed in the world of auctions, it could take much longer before that property starts having auctions. When a new property starts to have auctions, there are not a lot of people attending them in the first few months. The reason for this is **MOST** storage auction buyers are not information junkies. This is just another advantage of staying on top of your data. I bought a unit for $50.00 that made me $3600 because of this one step that I consistently undertook.

Knowledge is both power and money in the storage auction business.

It will take persistency and determination to build your storage auction database. In some extreme cases, you will have to drive to the storage facility and inquire about when the auctions will be held. I advise that you call early in the week because often on the day of the auction, you cannot reach anyone unless you have the back numbers, which I advise that you ask for once you are known as a regular. I cannot stress how important this is. By law, all storage businesses must advertise their auctions; you will gather all of the newspapers and this will work via legal organs for the areas that you will be buying your storage auctions in.

For example, here in Atlanta, www.dailyreport.com is the publication for these listings.

You will also cross-reference that information with the information that you are entering into your database. One question that I'm asked a lot is, **"should I buy a list of auctions or subscribe to an auction announcement service?"** My answer is no. Whether or not you have someone handing you the information of when auctions are going to occur, there still is a great deal of work that must be done. The announcements that come out at the beginning of the month will change. Let me state that again, that information will change drastically between the date it comes out in the paper or email and the day of the auction.

Why is this case?

It is a human tendency to wait until the last minute to handle business affairs. There are people that have the money to pay their storage auction bill but will wait until the very last minute to make the payment. That is why I say, if you are going to subscribe to an auction update service, just know the only benefit is you will know of some of the places that are having auctions and their dates. You will still have to pound the phone and do your due diligence. Because of the flaky nature of human beings many storage facilities that have 3–6 storage units listed for auction may, by the day of the auction, have one or none! Another thing that goes on is, the storage properties are making payment deals with the tenants, which means less units will be available for sale. Often, many of these deals are done minutes before the auction starts! It is a policy of many storage businesses to continue to call the delinquent tenant for payment right up to the time that the auction is supposed to start! The storage properties prefer to deal with the tenant first and you second or never. They make more money dealing with the tenant. That is the way the cookie crumbles and why you should always do your own home work. Once you develop a rapport with storage property managers, many will honestly tell you if it's worth it for you to come to that auction.

It is an ugly feeling to have a pocket full of money and head out to an auction that you find was canceled and you thought they were going to have ten units for sale. It happens frequently which is why it is so important for you to know where and when **ALL** of the auctions are happening in your area. This will ease a lot of uncertainly and apprehension. If all of your auctions are canceled on Monday, but you know there is a shit load of auctions on Tuesday, you take the day off and you're not driving all over town chasing your tail. Another thing about subscription services, by doing your own research you will find out that many do not include all of the auctions in your area! One of my webinar attendees told me that very fact; this is just another reason for you to do your own work. It will pay off more than you can know.

There will be a tendency to favor, what is termed *"the better neighborhoods."* Do not do that!

Recently, I put up a video of the storage property that I got the safe out of; it was a regular run of the mill neighborhood. Do not allow preconceived notions to infect your way of thinking. You can miss out on some really profitable storage auction units, thinking in this manner. I have bought okay units to awesome units in the hood! There's one thing that is very surprising about shopping in the hood—you tend to get a lot of scrap gold. Scrap gold is real gold that is dented or broken but it is still worth a lot of money. Many of my previous book buyers and students of my webinars seem to think that you're only going to get the better units in rich or well-to-do neighborhoods. If anything, the reverse is true! The reality of the situation is this; you can buy junk in any neighborhood and you can get great units in any neighborhood. As you go forward with building your information database, do not leave out any of the storage properties in your city.

The week before any big football game, there is a tremendous amount of hype and speculation. Sometimes, the talking heads are actually on point. Many times, they are so wrong it ain't funny. This is just to say, football teams have to play the game to see who's really going to win regardless of all the talk beforehand.

The same is true of storage properties. You should attend the auction first, wait at least a few times before making a decision to not keep this property on your list of auctions to attend. The criteria that you should use in making that determination should be based on the management of the property, not the property itself. To break that down, if the property manager shows certain tendencies that are not conducive to you getting good units at that property, you may want to remove them from your list. The property managers can influence whether a unit goes up for auction in many ways. From screwing up the placement of the legal ad, to purposely leaving a tenant out of the legal ad, misspelling their name, not having the correct address, the wrong phone number and so on, if any step is not properly done, the unit cannot be sold.

Over the years, I have noticed that when certain property managers left the property, the types of unit that went up for auction changed! Places that always had a few units started having several! Storage properties that only had junk started producing beautiful and profitable units! I noted early in my career, that the property manager had a tremendous amount of influence on the type of units that came up for auction. Many storage property senior management teams will refute that last statement. If you ask any seasoned storage auction buyer, they will confirm this with a quickness. If there is a glaring disparity in terms of how that property performs, the manager may not be there the next time you attend the auction. It seems to me, that a property manager or a district manager will be there for a short period of time, usually six months to two years or they will be around forever. Many storage auction personnel move around from company to company so it is not strange to see the better people running new storage businesses that enter the local market.

The Property Manager Profile

Property managers that hate auctions, consciously or subconsciously, frequently screw up the auction ads. I have seen this time and time again. Property managers that know what is in the unit from the roota to the toota often are going through the units themselves. When dealing with property managers that do not give a damn about the auctions, you tend to get your better units. In a word, the property managers have more power than you ever would know. For the most part, most property managers are decent and honest people just trying to earn a living. Many do their jobs well and can be an asset to you. Nevertheless, there is a segment that can be very damaging to your business and time. These people will become apparent in a very short period of time. Do not judge a book by its cover. Look, listen and discern. Then make your decision about the management.

What is Your Stack of Chips Looking Like Buddy?

Capital, how much do you have? Do you really know? This is a great business and it does not require a lot of upfront capital. However, it does require some capital. Can you get in this business with only $10.00?

Yes, you can. You will be able to buy some units and you will make some money. You also will be very frustrated. At the very minimum, you should have $500 as startup capital. $3000 would be ideal for a beginner.

"When most businesses cost, at a minimum, $75,000–$250,000 or more to open (this would be a very small business) that is tremendously cheap to enter a business."

As referenced previously, the ultimate is $10,000–$15,000 in startup capital. If you do not have that money initially, no problem—this is a business that you can organically fund. By sticking to the principles in this book, you can be at that operating capital level within two years. The biggest factor that will shape this process is how much free time you have available. The more time you have, the quicker you can get to this point. If you start off part time, it will take you longer. It all depends on your personal situation. I have one book buyer and webinar student that got to this point within eight months. He was in a great position; he had money saved and he was being paid unemployment benefits. Not many people would have bought my book and signed up for my webinar under those conditions. He continued to look for a job while doing the storage auction thing as a side gig. The first month that he made a $4000 profit, he stopped looking for a job and devoted all of his time and energy into the storage auction business.

Develop a budget and stick to it.

Rome was not built in a day and neither will you build your business that quickly! I strongly advise against using credit cards to buy units in the beginning before you have strong cash flow. There are many dangers to buying your auction units on credit and the first one listed is the most damaging!

Using credit cards to buy storage auction units, promotes overconfidence and bad decisions. A similar thing happens to people with too much cash on hand—they overspend and do not budget. Never, ever, gamble on a unit with a credit card as payment. When you spend cash, you pay more attention to what you're doing. There are a few storage auction buyers that I know, after watching these people for years, certain buying trends became evident. When one used his credit cards, his bidding was significantly higher and more frequent. When he had to use cash, his bidding was dramatically lower and less often.

This told me two things: 1.) he was operating on hope, and 2.) his business was not doing so well. If his business was doing well, he would have the cash to buy his units. He was hoping to get a big hit to balance out. Then, I notice that he disappeared for a few months, confirming my theory. You can get into a lot of trouble using your credit cards in the storage auction business.

When developing a budget, be realistic and include everything–gas, locks, anything and everything that you will use in your storage auction business. You want to keep track of all expenditures because you will be able to write this off, but you will need the proper documentation.

Many auctions are cash only, so it is a good practice to adopt. If you do use a credit card, call your credit card company in advance and advise them your charge activity may increase. If not, it's possible they may decline your charge.

That is a Lot of Shit to Move!

When you buy a unit, whether it's a small unit or large unit, there is always more stuff in there than you thought. This is the area that many people fall short. The logistics of this business will make you or break you. The logistics include things like moving it without damaging it and sorting it to sift out items that are unsuitable for resale. You must develop a process because sorting out units can be very time consuming. Once you buy and go through one large unit, either you will still love the business or you will get the hell out! Especially with your larger units like a 10 x 20 that is a complete household of stuff. If you buy that unit, you have to move it all and sort it all.

The first thing you should figure out is how you will move the units that you buy. Do you have a truck or cargo van? If you do have a truck, does it have a hitch? Can you drive a truck with a trailer? It is best if you already have a vehicle to move your items or at least have access to one. You can move quite a bit with a standard full size pickup truck and attached trailer, and many longtime storage auction buyer's use this setup. At a minimum, you will need a truck and a trailer. If you have a truck, you can rent a trailer from UHAUL very economically; there will be more about trucks and loading later in this book. Deal with your logistical issues now. Truck rentals are **EXPENSIVE!** Sometimes the unit is worth getting a rental and sometimes it isn't; it is all situational based.

Where are you going to store it?

Where are you going to process it? Your garage and basement will only hold so much. If that is your only place clean it up now! By the very nature of this business, you will accumulate a great deal of merchandise very quickly. If you are living in an apartment, there is a special chapter for you at the end of the book. Your requirements are unique and challenging, but you can still do it. Storage is a crucial part of the business; you're not going to sell everything immediately and you need a place to work to process your items. A two car garage can hold a lot of stuff if properly situated, but there are limitations with that method of warehousing. Regardless of whether you or a fulltime buyer or a part-time buyer, storage is an issue that you must solve in order to grow your business.

Are you going to hold them or fold them?

These are questions that you must ask yourself: are you all in? Do you want to do this full time? Are you a hobbyist? Are you a serial part timer?

The answer to these questions is very important. If you want to become a full-time professional storage auction buyer, but are not able to move forward with that ambition due to life circumstances at this juncture, that is not a problem. Write it down on your goal sheet and develop a process to get there. Not knowing what you want to do *is* very problematic. There will be many decisions that need to be made and without a clear course of action, you will stumble.

If you are uncertain of what direction you want to take, start off as a part time buyer and determine if you like the business or not. Once that question is answered, it becomes very easy to make the right decision. If you want to be a full-time storage auction buyer, the prepping will be different. To earn a significant income, you will need the proper tools. You absolutely must acquire a proper vehicle for loading and transporting, as soon as possible, if you do not have one. It will pay for itself quickly. The second thing is develop a plan to deal with your space issues. The larger your business becomes, the larger this issue will be. Solve this problem and money is almost guaranteed.

This business is unlike any other in that the more you buy the more money you will make. Do not take that as a blanket statement to buy each and every unit that you see. You want to acquire your units based on a plan of how well the items in those units fit the needs of your customer base. There is a lot to this business—many layers and nuances. There is a learning curve, and armed with the information in this book, that curve will be significantly flattened.

One of the reasons there's not a lot of information about storage auctions is the wide spread perception that you cannot make a lot of money as a storage auction **buyer unless you get lucky.** Nothing could be farther from the truth. With a system, a solid plan married to your determination and strong work ethic, you can do very well in this business. Another reason there's not a lot of information about this business is that for a very long period of time, it was exceptionally easy to make a lot of money—and the regulars kept their mouths shut.

When I first entered the business, there was almost a gypsy like atmosphere surrounding the environment. People looked funky and often spoke in hushed tones. It was abundantly clear, that I was an outsider during my first days in the business. They made it painfully clear; I was trespassing on their turf. Some of the regular storage auction buyers are eerily territorial. They will play with you, run you up and harass you to some degree. Most will silently tolerate you.

A lack of imagination is the ultimate reason there's not much information about storage auctions on the business side.

Life is what you make it!

You can become rich in this country hauling trash; it is a matter of scale and being super efficient on the logistical side of that business. The same concepts hold true in this business. After speaking with scores of people across the country and the fact that everyone remotely interested in the storage auction business finds my videos and blog, speaks volumes to the business process that I developed. In short, no one can do it like I did it and to date no one has even come close. Going forward, there will be many of you that will do it in the same manner that I did it and will become successful because of it. Some of you will exceed the money and success that I had. This is a wide open opportunity, full of all the critical components of an up and coming industry.

What Type of Income Can I Expect?

If you operate this business on a part-time basis, you can expect an income of $6000–$20,000 per year. These numbers are profit and would be higher if I included gross sales. I break it down to this level because this is the money that you get to keep and spend after your expenses are paid. Full time earnings are in the neighborhood of $35,000 to well over $100,000 a year. In order to reach this level, you will be running your business full time and attending auctions 4 to 5 days a week. You will have either a store and/or a warehouse. There are many ways that you can do this and I will break down each and every way, going forward in this book.

When you write your game plan down, I do **HIGHLY RECOMMEND WRITING YOUR PLAN DOWN IN A NOTEBOOK OR A DOCUMENT IN MS WORD AND REVIEW IT OFTEN!!!!**

5

Tools of the Trade

You can do a personal inventory and determine if you need to buy the following items, many of which you may have laying around the house. There is no need to spend a lot of money to get in this business. Take your time and buy the items as you need them.

Work Gloves—I like the leather ones but you should use what is most comfortable to you. Some storage units are very clean, most are not. It can be something as simple as dust that has accumulated over the years. Yes, some people store stuff for years! You want to protect yourself and keep your hands clean for when you are logging items on your laptop.

Heavy Duty Trash Bags—the contractor type works best. Why would you need trash bags? Oh, let me count the ways. The average unit that I have bought, suffers from some of these common packing and moving faux pas—the first one being the most common. Instead of taping the box together, some people will fold the flaps of the box in the interlocking pattern. This will hold very light items, not dishes. Unfortunately, I cannot recall how many boxes that I have picked up and the bottom of the box completely comes apart and all of the contents fall to the floor of the storage unit.

Another common and sad method of moving is the *"Georgia Suitcase Method."* This is when there is not one box in the unit! This person moved all of their possessions in trash bags—very cheap and flimsy trash bags that rip apart as soon as you touch them. It is more efficient and speedy to scoop these items up and placed in a heavy duty trash bag. Time is money; the sooner you can get the stuff cleaned out, the sooner you can start making money. By the way, when this happens to you and it will, it's perfectly natural to be pissed and cuss.

Packing Tape and unassembled boxes—keep a few rolls of packing tape and boxes with you in your truck or van; this is the same issue above, with totally different requirements. I have pulled out a very valuable vase that was in a trash bag. People will pack their belongings in the strangest manner.

Old Blankets or quilts—for padding the furniture or as packing material. Sometimes, you will have everything that you need to pack up your items in the unit. On occasion, you will have to supplement or you run the risk of damaging your furniture.

Rope or Straps—if you have a box truck, it is best to leave the ropes and straps tied to the slats of the box truck. These are items that you will use frequently, to keep the items in a less than full truck from moving around.

Locks —you get your best deals on locks in Wal-Mart. They offer for sale three to four lock packs keyed the same. Go with mid grade to high security locks. I favor disc locks because they are hard to break into, but you want to get a mixture of locks. All storage property unit door latches are not the same and you will not be able to place your disc lock on those latches. When the auction is going on, people get excited— so excited they forget their locks. There've been many issues of a person buying a unit, not locking it and later on finding things missing. As soon as you get out of the car, make sure you have your locks with you. After winning a storage auction unit, immediately place your lock on it. It is far better to be safe than sorry.

High Intensity Spot Light—some people choose to carry the spotlight and others do not. My preference is to carry one, they save you money or they make you money. I will give you an example, once I was getting ready to drop the hammer down and buy this unit. Just before I was about to place my last bid, I saw that the headboard of a beautiful bedroom set, was cracked right down the middle. I stopped bidding on it and the other person got it. Later on, I learned that many items in a unit were damaged. If I had won that unit with my last bid, I would have lost my ass. **This is a case of a spotlight saving you money**.

Another example, I was at an auction that was taking place inside a climate control building. Sometimes the lighting is very poor inside these buildings. It was a 10 x 20 storage unit that was packed from the roota to the toota and it was somewhat difficult to determine the value of the unit. I got on my hands and knees, shined my light on the bottom of the unit and saw the tires of a motorcycle. I took my time getting up, actually acted as if my knees hurt. If I got up too quickly, someone may have caught on. I ended up getting the unit for $520. If any of those other guys had seen the motorcycle tires, that unit would have cost me $2000 or more. I sold the bike for $1800.

This is an example of how a light can make you money and a lesson on how to use your light. It was a very good unit. I suggest a spotlight with candlepower in the range of one-two million candle power range, not a flash light. Flashlights are not strong enough and you can get spotlights at Wal-Mart or Target for $25–$35 dollars. As a side note, some of the lights are very heavy.

Smart Phone—with 7 megapixel camera or better. The pictures my EVO takes are phenomenal! If you do have one currently and your contract is not up anytime soon you can get one at a great price off of Craigslist—there is a robust mobile phone market there. The reason for having a smart phone is so you can have access to vital information on the spot. Most smart phones allow you to surf the Internet; you can get real time information during an auction to help you make a decision to buy the unit or not to buy unit. If conditions are right, you can take a picture of the item you just bought using your smart phone. Then proceed to place the item for sale in one of your sales channels before you go to the next auction. I wish this was available during the early days of my storage auction career.

A 7-10 Megapixel Camera—high quality pictures sell items much better than crappy low quality pictures. This is your calling card—don't skimp. I have sold many items over the internet because of the high quality pictures alone!

Gmail Accounts—the best free email account ever! One of the best features of a Gmail account is the unlimited storage. You'd never have to delete an e-mail; this is a great thing for your business. Another very important reason you must have a Gmail account is to take advantage of the Picasa online photo album feature. There will be more about this in the selling section.

Photobucket.com—I have used Photobucket for years, with great success. This is a great resource for your business because you can super size your items for sale in your pictures and make more of an impact in your sales presentation. A picture does say a thousand words.

Computer—preferably, one for your business and a separate one for the family to avoid conflicts that will arise! This will be your best friend. You want to have a reliable computer because a large percentage of your business will be initiated and conducted online.

Internet Connection—high speed baby! You will be uploading a lot of pictures. If it is not available in your area, just make do with what you have.

eBay accounts—yes, accounts. You can have as many as you like as long as they do not interact with each other. Start with two and add more as your business increases. The reason that you want to have multiple eBay accounts is, eBay has become very Calvinist in their behavior towards sellers.

You want to have your main "shotgun" account that you sell any and everything on. For your nicer, name brand high end items, you want to start developing the feedback reputation for selling those types of things. eBay will limit your account in a heartbeat; their rationale is if you do not have a history of selling a certain type of item, you are dangerous and should be treated as such. The catch–22 is, as a new seller, you have no history but that does not mean that you are a crook!

Sell as much as you can on both eBay accounts, this will diminish the chances of you getting limited later on. If you do not currently have an eBay account, and you start selling a lot of items and making a lot of money, expect a phone call/your account to be limited.

I do not agree with the way they handle the situations. It is my belief that this vetting process should occur on the front end not while you're in the middle of making money. I know this may sound like I am being overly pessimistic, I am not. As a storage auction buyer you can purchase a unit tomorrow that will make you $10,000–$15,000, or more, very quickly on eBay. This has happened to me on more than one occasion. I bought a unit and everything in that unit was perfectly suited to sell on eBay.

I did very well with sales immediately and I immediately ran into a problem with eBay and PayPal. eBay deleted all of my auctions and suspended my account. PayPal placed a hold on all of my funds. I was contacted by both eBay and PayPal and was asked to submit a ton of documentation; my driver's license and social security number, which I did— they had me by the balls.

I did everything that they asked and within 24 hours my selling privileges were restored and PayPal released the hold on my money. That was a nerve wracking day! They were at one point holding $12,000 of my money and most of the merchandise had been shipped out! Please do not take this advice lightly when dealing with eBay and PayPal. As long as you just sell a few things here and there, and never make what I consider significant money, you may never ever have a problem with eBay and PayPal. I went through this song and dance with both of them a total of six times!

You would think after the first time I would not have to go through this type of validation process. Alas, that is not the case. Any time that you change the items that you sell or as an eBay representative told me over the phone, switch categories, the clock starts ticking all over again. Regardless of your sparkling clean record, huge spikes in volume and payments will make eBay and PayPal nut up like a Klansman at a Jay Z concert. My history with both leads me to believe that MOST people are not making a generous income on eBay, otherwise they would not behave in such a Gestapo like manner when ones' income goes up —that is the whole point of selling your items on eBay—to make money! With that said, in spite of their crazy antics and insipid behavior at times, eBay hands down is the best place to sell unique, rare and certain valuable merchandise. After many lawsuits, their behavior is much better these days.

PayPal Account—they get a little weird if you have more than one business and one personal account, however, you can do it legally. When you start a business under a corporate entity (Inc or LLC) this is a new financial being with its own tax ID number. By incorporating or setting up an LLC, you can open a PayPal account in the name of the business. Do you think Dell, IBM and other corporations have a person signing up for their PayPal and eBay accounts? No, they're not. It is a little tricky and most of the PayPal representative will not know what you are talking about.

It can be done; I've accomplished it two times. As of this writing, you can still do it but know that this may change any day. I would not advise anyone to set up a corporation to gain another PayPal account. Setting up LLCs and incorporating is expensive and comes with a certain level of responsibilities that you do not need if you do not have a real business. You will need a separate address and phone number. Your address and phone number must be in databases in order to be approved for your corporate PayPal account. They will run a Dun & Bradstreet report on you (DNB is a business credit reporting company) and if you're not in DNB, more than likely, they will not approve your account. Setting up a business credit profile, is a book in itself.

Open your PayPal account now, this way you can get your PayPal debit card after two months of having a fully active PayPal account. You must fulfill all of the requirements before getting a debit card from PayPal; this makes getting paid a breeze. You can withdraw up to $400 daily from ATM's and make purchases of up to $3000 per day using it as a credit card. This can be very handy when you're out at auctions, to have money coming in that you can readily access and buy more merchandise with. There has been many a day where I went out to auctions with $1500–

$3000 and by lunch time, I had an additional $3000 or more to spend at auctions. That is the beauty of making money online, it can happen any day and any hour—which is a grand thing.

Major Online Book Sellers (Amazon)—I feel that registering with major online book sellers provides a great source of passive income. As a storage auction buyer, you will come across many books, CDs and DVDs. By selecting the best books and media to place on **major online book seller** sites, you will create very good passive income over time. I call this passive income because you're not attempting to become a major online book seller– seller. It is a byproduct of an action that you are already doing.

By setting minimum listing criteria, you will avoid the penny books and CD syndrome. Our minimum threshold was $3.00 for CD's and DVD's and $7.00 for books. The reason it was set up like this is twofold. Many major online book sellers take 25% of the sale of an item right off the top and you must foot the bill for shipping until you're remunerated later on in the month. Essentially, since this was an indirect form of income it had to be worth the fees and the time to ship. Our passive income major online book seller account was making $2800–$3600 per month based on the criteria that I just gave you. When you buy a lot of units, you will gain several hundred to thousands of books per month. Some of those books will be very profitable!

Google Voice Number—they are free, just go to Google voice to apply or get an invite. It used to be Grand Central. It is a cool way to have a business number and every time it rings, you know it is about money! Another reason to have this service is for safety and anonymity. All landlines and mobile phones are listed in readily accessible databases. The majority of these databases are free and anyone can gain your personal information, such as your home address and name. With a Google Voice number that all goes away; Google is the only entity that knows you have the number. If you know anything about Google, they are not real big on giving out company information!

Craigslist Account—Craigslist is always changing things—sometimes you need an account to post an item, sometimes you do not. Craigslist is an exceptional resource for your business. As a high volume seller you will need your own Craigslist accounts—yes, accounts. I currently have four Craigslist accounts. You will need that many if you're moving a significant amount of merchandise. I love Craigslist so much that I wrote a book about it that goes into great detail on how to make money on Craigslist:

Pimping Craigslist For Fun and Profit

Here is a quick overview on how to sell on Craigslist (I go into far more detail in the book). Craigslist is a wonderful place, but it is like the wild, wild west—a true democracy. There is a certain art to making your ad stand out and if you have never used Craigslist to sell an item, now is the time to practice. You'll develop an addiction, as so many others who use Craigslist for the first time do.

When someone calls you from Craigslist, it is in your best interest to answer the call. They have too many options and you can lose sales by taking your time getting back to people. I am not saying take phone calls at 1:00 am in the morning; yes they do call at that time! Just get back to them as soon as you possibly can. I usually took calls from 7:00 am to 8:30 pm.

If the item is small enough to put in your car, meet them in public. If you allow them in your home, have someone with you. I have never had a funky encounter, but I am a rather large guy, this could be different for a woman doing this. Just take heed, I never met anyone late at night; use some common sense when you're dealing with people on Craigslist. Overall, using Craigslist to sell items is worth the hassle!

Priced right you can sell many an item the same day. This is going to take a little work but you MUST research your item and price it accordingly or it will languish and you will have to relist it over and over. If you place a bedroom set on Craigslist for twelve hundred dollars without knowing the market value, it is to your disadvantage. The same bedroom set is new in the store selling for one thousand dollars. You are wasting your time which we all know is very precious. Know the market. Faster sales equal faster profits!

Earlier in the book, I made reference to the fact that you should know where you want to take this business. Whether you will be part time are at some point in the future fulltime. If you are seriously thinking that this will be a fulltime endeavor for you, there are certain steps that you need to take now.

Doing The Legal Thing

If renting a building or warehouse is part of your plans I suggest you take the following steps for your business. Incorporate or form a LLC (**Limited Liability Corporation**). Go to your Secretary of State for details on how to do this—it is not hard and there is no reason to pay someone $500-$600 to do it for you. In Georgia you can form a LLC online for $100. I would suggest the LLC unless you are going to sell shares of your company then you would need a traditional incorporation, which is more complex than an LLC and requires additional steps to form. Consult a tax professional on this based on your situation.

Part of this process is deciding what you're going to name your business entity. Think about that before you start filling out forms. If you think you have a great name concept, you might want to protect it. If you have the inclination and the capital, consult professionals in this arena. There are far too many things that can go wrong that will impact your company. I am neither a CPA nor an attorney; consult these professionals before you press forward with name protections and trademarks. If you do not have the money, the information is readily available online and in your local library. I suggest a copious amount of due diligence before you do anything. The next step after you have determined your Company name, decide which business entity you would use for your business and apply for a Taxpayer EIN which is like a Social Security number for your business, it is not but it will be used as such. They are free to obtain from the IRS.

How to get your Employee Identification Number:

http://www.irs.gov/businesses/small/article/
0,,id=97860,00.html

Open a business checking account after getting your EIN;
they are free in most areas. Apply for a resale license or
certificate. This is not a business license—this certificate
gives you a resale number and you can use it to buy items at
wholesale costs, without paying sales tax. You may need a
business license to get into certain wholesale
establishments, always check before showing up!

Apply for a business credit card or you may be able to
convert one of your personal cards to a business credit
card. Note—do not use this card to buy auctions—it is just
a tool for your business profile. Business credit cards do
not have the same built in protections as personal credit
cards. Just be wary when using any credit card for this
business. Now that you are all set up it is much easier to
see where your money is going or how your income is
progressing. Do not commingle funds, it will get very
confusing and you cannot get a true picture of your
business's health. Always track your money; I did it weekly,
making end of the month accounting a breeze! Okay, you
have your goals, your game plan in hand, you know where
the auctions are so, are you ready to buy?

Nope!

There is much more to do! Getting yourself ready for the
business is more about planning and attitude than anything
else. The first thing is getting your home or office ready for
what is to come. I know I mentioned it before, but this will
be the weak link; you will run out of space quicker than you

think! Many times you have the option to rent the unit, but it is very hard to sort and process your inventory in the unit. Note this can really cut into your profits several ways. First of all, you may have to pay the full rent on the unit. Everyone does not offer discounts of rental specials. If this unit is far from your home you need to factor in the fuel cost and then there is your personal time in "working the unit".

All of these costs must be factored in on the final balance sheet. Expenses like these are what I term "leakage". Many people in the auction business only factor in hard costs—the cost of the unit, eBay fees, PayPal fees and whatever cost you may incur in the buying and selling of the unit. It should be noted that if you buy an okay unit, this means you will not make a huge profit and the slim margin units will kill you! Keep a small note book with you to chart these costs on your main spreadsheet. If you are going to file taxes **(I highly recommend it)** the cost of going to auctions is fully deductible. See a tax professional to chart out your plan.

Sometimes, working out of a unit makes taking pictures clearly impossible. There are times it will work, say the unit is half empty or it is a unit of lumber or fixtures that you are going to sell to a company and they will pick it up. There are other situations where it will work and some of you may not have a choice because of the lack of space. It was very frustrating for me to do it, which is why I gave it up fairly quickly. When you buy a unit there will be some items you do not want to keep—do not let that be a determent. Here is a way to get rid of stuff—as long as it is usable, donate it at fair market value and take it off your taxes. As an individual, you will run into your donation limit quite quickly. If you have a business, you can donate a lot more. We usually donated fifty thousand dollars a year, of stuff we could not sell, to Good Will and other charities.

At the end of the book there is a special section for apartment dwellers.

There is another way to free yourself of unwanted and unsellable items—it is the free section of Craigslist. Mixed in some units are some items that you know you are not going to make much money on so you put it up on Craigslist. I have gotten rid of so much stuff in this manner that it is ridiculous! As you build your business you will find out there are some things you just need to sell ultra cheap to move it. Use the dump for the totally trashed items. Some waste companies allow you to dump for free—others will charge based on tonnage. Where you live in the country will make the difference on this one.

If you are building a large organization, you may want to have one of those haul containers in the back of your business. It is very convenient and the costs are the same if you are going to the dump once a week with large loads. One thing to be aware of is that people will go through your dumpsters large or small. Sometimes they make a mess and sometimes they do not.

Nothing pissed me off more than going around to the back of my business and seeing trash all around the dumpster! Just a note of one of the nuances of owning a store; I got to the point where I started locking the dumpster. I really do not care if someone wants something out of the trash but I do care if I have to spend thirty minutes or more at the beginning of my day cleaning up my place!

Here is another thing you can do to get rid of stuff you don't want—there are usually guys at the auctions who do not have much money and will clean out the units for you if you give them a few good things in return for their service. I have used six of these guys with no issues. Usually the ones who have it in their blood and are at every auction will be your best bet. Have a firm understanding with these people because the onus is on **"you"** to get the unit cleaned out. I was always present during the loading on this type of arrangement that way I was sure the stuff was removed.

Did you do the following?

Open up your eBay, PayPal and **major online book seller** accounts yet? No?

WHY NOT? Let me run this scenario by you—**AGAIN!!!!**

You get some really good eBay suitable stuff in your first unit or a ton of books for cheap! You take all your stuff home and put it online and it starts selling like crazy. All is going well, and then it happens. You get an email from PayPal asking you for more information about yourself and your business. Or the phone call from PayPal which, if you do not answer, they will limit your account immediately! This has happened to me six different times! Changing categories prompts their attention, if you sell a lot of stuff in a short period of time, if you are new, if you open a new account with the same information as the old account, it does not matter. They go nuts on any rapid swing where you are making more money! Their official policy is to shoot first and ask questions later! This can ruin your sales and induce customers to lose confidence in you! What did you do wrong? Absolutely nothing!

There is nothing like that feeling in the pit of your stomach of utter helplessness! Hence the reason I became a rebel. I always had more than one eBay account and more than one PayPal account for these very reasons! Because you are brand new and selling well—which means you are making a lot of money—you are all up in their radar! Which means your money can be locked up in their systems for years! Nope, there's nothing you can do about it because you agreed to this when you signed up for the account per their terms of service agreement.

Before the eBay veterans chime in, understand when this happened to me I went from four thousand dollars in sales a month to twenty thousand dollars in three weeks. If your selling volume jumps tremendously, they will review you! They may even take all your auctions down and make you submit documentation about your business. If you have been on there for a while and are actively selling, you **MAY** be okay. If you are a **veteran ebayer** you know things are always changing on the site. It is just a part of the business.

I would not bet any money on eBay letting you take a pass on a large increase in sales just because you have some history. I would definitely take precautions! To circumvent all of this, now is the time to open an eBay and PayPal account and start selling the items in your house that you do not need to build up a reputation with eBay and PayPal.

Life is what you make it!

This is the only way you are going to sell certain items for maximum profit. It is best to know the rules of engagement before you begin.

Beginning now also frees up space for the stuff that you are going to buy. Does that make sense? Another bonus is, if you do not have much money to spare to buy units, this is a great way to build up your operating funds. Yes, I mentioned this before; I just thought it was worth repeating.

Many **major online book sellers** will limit new sellers, so if you are an old seller you will not have this problem. Out of the three platforms mentioned, a **major online book seller** is probably the most straight forward online platform to sell items on. So begin now!

6

Dipping Your Toe in the Water

For your first foray into the storage auction business, scope out a day that has several auctions going on. People are notorious for paying late which means the auction may be canceled minutes before it begins, so have some backups, some options, if you will. You want to know EVERY AUCTION, yes every auction that is going on that day. This is the secret ingredient; most folks are too lazy to obtain this information. They will ask you if you know of any other auctions going on today. I am a big-time advocate of doing your own work. You can catch some killer deals on this tactic alone.

I know you are a kind soul, but do not share your info. It would be a pity for you to lose out on a good auction unit because you told someone about an auction they did not even know was happening! I did it. Once. I was new and being an information junkie I knew what properties were having an auction and where they were every day of the week. I kept this information on an excel spreadsheet along with property phone numbers and the auctioneers or managers phone number. The auction we were waiting on to start was canceled, so I whipped out my sheet to see where the next nearest auction was. One guy I did not know saw the sheet and came up to me and said "cool, can I look at it?"

Like a dumbass I honored his request. Later on I started doing my research in my van or sneaking off quietly. We both set off to the auction; there were only two other people there when we arrived. We see two okay units and then Ooooooooooooooooo a mother–load unit. A 10 X 40 stacked from the roota to the toota (front to back and to the ceiling). I mean just jammed packed! Clean stuff too! You could see part of four bedroom sets, the dining room set— essentially furnishings from a very large home was in that unit. A very nice stately home!

I started bidding and the two people who were there first said that was way too much stuff for them to handle. I am smiling and thinking I am golden! I opened my bid at one hundred dollars. Well guess who starts bidding? Yep, my new found friend! I am like what the hell? I look at him *"what gives dude?"* He said *"this is too good to pass up!"* We go and go higher and higher three hundred, four hundred, five hundred, one thousand, twelve hundred, fifteen hundred then he jumps the bid to eighteen fifty! I end up getting the unit for nineteen hundred dollars, when if I had kept my big mouth closed I would have gotten it for one hundred dollars. Fortunately it was a jackpot unit and well worth the money, but I could have been eighteen hundred dollars up, if I was not so freaking helpful.

You could say I became a little jaded at that point. I was pissed at myself and I never gave anyone a tip again. This ass, which I saw weeks later at another auction, had the inimitable gall to ask me where some more auctions were happening as soon as he saw me.   No, he was not the sharpest knife in the drawer. "I do not know dog, I have no clue," was all I said to him from that point. on.

I've even had people follow me; this is where I have taken people on wild goose chases! After a while I was known for being the guy in the know and people would ask me all of the time what was going on. All I can say is subterfuge and misdirection. I would stop at a Quiktrip and drive round and round through all of the gas pumps with the people following me! Then gun it out the exit just as the light is changing. Any large service station will do! Go to a fast food place park, go inside, order your food to go and dip while they are in line! Some auction vets would wait until the parking lot was empty before going to the next sale. Once a guy was following me and he ran a red light trying to keep up with me! I am about to fall out of my chair as I write this, oh the memories! If someone asked me if I was going to the next auction I usually would say okay, but if you just start following me, I will take you on a ride, if I have the time!

There were a few times I was going home and they thought I was going to another auction. This would prompt me to pull over and tell them I was done for the day. I did not want these people to know where I lived! In a word, keep your cards close to the vest. The other people may be nice, talk to them, make friends but understand that everyone at the auction is your competition and when it comes down to dollars and friends the dollars win most of the time.

Some of the things you can expect to find in a unit

I am often asked what you can find in a storage unit. The sun, earth and moon...perhaps even a bathroom sink. Okay, all of that stuff was some kid's science project...

Just pause for a moment and look around your current surroundings and whatever you see, more than likely is in a storage unit. The large majority of items are from residential homes or just excess storage of things like Christmas decorations, grand ma antiques, books or whatever you need to hold on to for legal reasons.

Many businesses use storage units to store inventory, records, raw materials and some businesses are even run out of storage units. I know one place where this really nice shoe store in Buckhead has two 12 x 40's full of new shoes. Yes, I made a point to look every month to see if those units were coming up for auction. If you get deeply vested in this business you will start noting a unit's contents. When you are at the auction, many times you see people working in their units or moving in. I have gotten a few but not many of those units. It does pay to keep mental notes. It is also a good practice to learn how to know the sizes of the units— they are fairly standard. 5x5—half a closet, 5 x 10—a small walk in closet, 10 x 10—divide a two car garage into four spaces, with the quarter being the size of a 10 x 10, 10x 15, 10 x 20 enough space for four cars stacked on top of each other and 10 x 30 or 10 x 40 think RV size. I have actually seen an antique fire truck in a 10 x 40. Some storage facilities will modify a unit for you. Say take down a wall and turn two 10 x 20s into a 20 x 40! That is a lot of stuff! I have gotten a few and if it is full it will take two moving trucks to get it all or two to three trips to move it all.

This is my list of the items that you will more than likely find in a storage unit.

Appliances

Albums

Antiques

Automobiles

Art work—bought and original

Brooms—tons of brooms

Bedroom Sets

Boxes

Books

Bookcases

Bolts

Bibles

Brakes—yes, car brakes

Car parts

Collectibles

Cable boxes—damn near every room in some parts of town

Cereal

Computers

Cash or change

Clothing

Life is what you make it!

Cards—playing, greeting, school

Cases

Cables

Coins

Construction equipment

CD's

DVD's

Doors

Dog Cages

Drugs—prescription and illegal both can be problematic

Electrical equipment

Food—hate it with a passion! Attracts rodents!

Furniture

Guns

Gold

Inventory

Ink

Jewelry

Kitchen stuff

Lawn Mowers

Ladders

Lights

Lamps

Laundry

Mannequins

Movies

Mirrors

New Stuff

Pianos

Pools

Pool Tables

Roaches

Rats

Shoes

Shocks

Signs

Saws

Tires

Tools

Tools Boxes

Tractors

Wheels

Life is what you make it!

Urns—with ashes

This is a small list; there is no limit to what you may find in a storage unit. I just listed a few common things so you can gain a perspective of what you are getting yourself into. This can easily become a lifestyle! I know several people who no longer buy new anything other than food. I will be honest; ninety percent of my clothing came out of units. I have often come across a unit where the guy was my size and got a new wardrobe for ten to a hundred dollars and I am talking new with tags!

Everything that I am wearing in the **Youtube.com/ glendon007** videos came out of storage units! Not to brag but my gear is "fly!" Shoes, watches, and cufflinks you name it I got it out of storage units. If you work it just right you can make money and save money in the storage auction business. I have and so can you! Let's talk about guns. This is a very sensitive item that you can get out of a storage unit.   I will say use caution to the upmost. All states are different in regards to what you can and cannot do with a gun that you got out of a storage unit.

Long guns or rifles tend to not be as problematic as pistols or handguns. If you get one, know the laws of your state before you do anything with that gun. Don't be Plexico Burress with his dumbass!

In Georgia, you can sell guns fairly easily as long as it is not stolen. There is a GUN SHOW every month in the Atlanta area; you may have something like that in your neck of the woods.   You have got to check the status of the gun before you sell it. Selling a stolen gun will cost you a lot of money and perhaps some jail time. It is not worth the risk! You need to befriend a cop and have him run the numbers; if it comes up hot more than likely he is going to have to turn it in. If you get a fully automatic weapon out of a unit do not tell anyone until you figure out if it is stolen. Just having one without the proper paper work is a ten thousand dollar fine and possible jail time! All states do not allow the possession or use of fully automatic weapons for non law enforcement personal, so you must be careful with this one. I am not saying I had some, but if I did, this is what I would do. First, call from a pay as you go phone, ask the local police department to ascertain if this weapon was stolen— let them run the check on the serial number. If not, there are several gun dealers who can and will buy this weapon from you. Go online and inquire.

DO NOT HAVE THIS WEAPON IN YOUR CAR WHILE YOU ARE JUST RIDING AROUND. WITH AMMO OR NOT YOU CAN GO TO JAIL IF YOU GET PULLED OVER FOR THAT ROUTINE TRAFFIC STOP!

Once you find a dealer and he is clear that it is not stolen, take the gun to the dealer and he can buy it from you or sell it for you. Only a licensed gun dealer can legally ship guns to another licensed gun dealer for the buyer to pickup. I would not even think to try to the skirt the system on this one. If the gun comes up stolen, you can turn it in or toss it. Know that if you turn it in, they are going to want to go through the rest of the unit. Maybe even seize the unit to conduct an investigation, so my friend these are your choices. By the way, I have never had a unit seized.

Life is what you make it!

If you toss it, break it apart (all automatic weapons break apart) make it inoperable and wear gloves while you are doing this. You should be good to go. Yes, this is destroying evidence, but if you keep your mouth closed and do not tell anyone, who will know? It is your choice. Sensitive item number two are drugs— prescription or illegal—either one can land you in jail. So be careful, this is why I stopped sorting on site.

I bought a unit, my first year in the business, near downtown Atlanta. I loaded it all in the van and headed out. Not a good one hundred yards away from the storage facility I hit a pot hole and a bag of weed pops out of a box into the front of the van. A sandwich bag full of weed and I do mean full. Can you say possession with intent to distribute? I almost had a liquid moment. As soon as I got home I flushed it. Later on, some of my friends who, unbeknownst to me were pot heads became very upset potheads once I told them what I had and where I got it. It is a sad thing to see a pot head cry; apparently the West End has the best weed in town—who knew?

Sensitive item number three; stolen merchandise. What are the chances of you getting stolen goods? Medium to pretty high, depending upon where you are buying. Chances of getting caught, slim to none. If they knew where the stuff was it would never go up for auction. Then you have the burden of proof. I never had a problem. Automobiles and motorcycles are stored in units. Most storage facilities check on the cars to see if a lien is in place before the sale. If there is a lien they turn it in to the lien-holder. If there is no lien, they let the sale proceed. Say you get a car at auction. How can you sell it with no paperwork?

How to Obtain Paperwork for Cars!

Sometimes the title is in the unit. Just take that title to your local DMV with your receipt and usually they will give you a title in your name. I have only done it six times, it may be different now. It all depends on your state and the requirements to get a title. If there is no title, you can get what is called a Bonded Title. If you do not have acceptable evidence of ownership for your vehicle; you have the option of applying for a bonded title.

In order to qualify for a bonded title, you must be a resident or military personnel stationed in that state; or have a vehicle that was last titled in that state. The vehicle must be in your possession and cannot be considered abandoned, junked, stolen, or involved in pending lawsuits. Although not required to be operational, it must be a complete vehicle including a frame, body and motor or frame and motor if a motorcycle. This usually costs a little over a hundred dollars to obtain.

The bond title will be obtained from the state that you live in; it can be a simple process or a lengthy process! You must establish that you are the owner of the vehicle and may need to have it appraised by an insurance adjuster. Call up your DMV and inquire about their application process.

7

Ready, Aim, Fire!
Let's go to a Storage Auction

Today is the day, your first auction!

Aren't you excited? Who knows what you will see! Make sure you have your cash, locks, excel spreadsheet, spot light, trash bags, gloves, old blankets, rope, and tape in your vehicle (if you are driving your loading vehicle), if not just have your locks and loot to buy units. Always keep your business plan in mind; it is a good idea to review it every day! Wear old clothes or work clothes to the auction. If you buy something you want to be prepared. Have the cash on your person; many times you will not be given an opportunity to go to the bank. Things can be fast paced on auction day.

You may want to carry a gun!

If you go to a lot of auctions you will develop a habit of carrying a lot of cash. If may freak you out at first! I packed a .45 that I got out of a unit. Yes, it was legal! Just a bit of advice for you, park across the street or on the edge of the parking lot of the storage facility. In the event of large turn outs, you do not want to be blocked in, just in case you need to run to another auction! Once you get to know your crowd, sometimes it makes sense to go to another auction when you know most folks are at the one you just left. I have been known to turn around and go to a less crowded auction in a heartbeat and gotten killer deals. Sneak off quietly, usually when everyone is looking at a unit you can walk off unnoticed.

I cannot emphasize enough how important it is to know what is going on in your city in terms of auction schedules. Build your own database—it will be worth more than gold!

Get to know the people and managers, good relationships can go a long way in this business. When they get to know you, there are benefits not extended to new bidders. You can save extra time by calling ahead and sometimes they will call you if a tenant is about to become delinquent and just wants to liquidate the unit.

There are a lot of perks to being an auction hound! Call when enroute to check on cancellations. So many people pay late so it is a good policy in case you need to divert yourself to another auction on your sheet.. After you sign in, ask the property manager how long the unit has been rented for. Most people do not rent self storage units for two or more years to store junk, in some cases it does happen— there are always exceptions to any rule—most people however do not. Don't get upset if they do not know, the turnover in this business is pretty high when it comes to staff at the storage facility.

Arrive fifteen to thirty minutes ahead of time. Some auctioneers will lock you out of the auction if you are even one minute late. Be sure to have your locks on you. You will be amazed at how many people come to the auction with no locks; they really are not that serous about it.

The Auctions is on!

Usually, before auctioning the first unit, the auctioneer or storage facility manager will go over the rules. Included in this speech is how long you have to clean out the unit, if it is cash only or if they take credit cards, whether you can smoke or not, if there is sales tax, if you can or cannot rent the unit after purchase, to leave the personal effects at the office (pictures, bibles, business papers, tax records essentially stuff you cannot sell), and how the bidding is conducted. Someone may tell a few jokes and it is on! We are ready to go. Your first thing to do is get as close to the door as possible. If there is a large crowd, some people will block the door and the auction can be over before you even see the unit. Be polite but firm and work your way toward the front. Some auctioneers will not let the bidding start until everyone has seen the contents of the unit. This is not always the case so you have to go with the flow.

If you did your research beforehand, you will know if one person has two or more units up for auction. Think very large homes. Sometimes it is in the paper, sometimes they are in different names. As you are looking over the units, if you see something that looks like it matches the items you have seen just before in another unit they may be cousins!

I once bought three units in Dunwoody that belonged to the same person. I did not know these units belonged to the same person until we loaded the units and things started matching up from different units! One had the glass for the sofa table, the chair cushions were in two different units and so on. There were no obvious clues that all of this stuff belonged to the same person! It happens, that is why it is a good policy to inquire.

If you get the first part, you more than likely will need the other unit. We call these two-fers or three-fers and it happens a lot so just be on the lookout for it when you are buying. If you don't think you have enough cash to get both of the units, leave it alone. There are a lot of assholes out there who will not work with you and neither one of you can realize a full profit potential on the units. I have never been in this position, but it can bite! I have seen the bad blood that develops over it.

This is a contest and you have to be aggressive. If there are not a lot of people at the auction, be very thorough. Take a good look at the boxes. Are they taped up? Have they been retaped? Did this person move the items with friends or did a moving company do it? This is a biggie, check for odors; people often store food, chemicals, gas and other things that produce smells in storage units. Food brings rodents; sometimes you will see the droppings.

I know gross! Right?

Well if you are a brave soul, these units make money, because most people walk away as soon as the aroma hits the air! I have gotten these types of units for ten dollars! We are talking ten by twenties, which is essential enough stuff to fill up a three or four bedroom home. Remember the trash bags on the list? Throw the crap away and sell the good stuff!

Life is what you make it!

One note on sofas and love seats—count the cushions if you can. For some strange reason people will keep the cushions and you cannot sell it without cushions. Forget about having cushions made, unless you can do it yourself. It is ridiculously expensive to have cushions made. We are talking one hundred or more dollars per cushion!

Check out the legs of the furniture. Often the family pooch uses tables and furniture legs as a chew toy, which just kills the value of the furniture. Look for the glass in china cabinets, is it in the furniture or is it off to the side? Poster bed finials are crucial to getting a good price on a rice bed or poster bed. You can still sell these beds without the finials, but it is usually for cheap! Often you can find the finial in a corner or cabinet, sometimes they just leave them on the bed. Often they are broken, but that is an easy fix with a drill and another anchor screw.

The same thing goes with dressers, nightstands and chests. If the drawers are not in the cased goods, (dressers, chest and china cabinets) look for them if you can. Sometimes they are not in the unit but in that place far, far, away! Yes! They are in never, never land—that strange place where it is best to store the item, versus keeping it with the furniture it was made to fit.

On the subject of drawers, learn to tell the difference between particle board and real wood furniture. It is critical. Particle board furniture doesn't move very well nor is the resale on it that great. It is usually pretty easy to note the difference; however, when the adrenaline is rushing through your veins it can cloud your judgment.

Big units stacked very neatly are usually the sign of a moving company whether you see moving company boxes are not. Many well organized people start boxing up stuff weeks in advance of the move and use whatever boxes they can get their hands on. There are no hard and fast rules on this, just look for the common theme; is it the same handwriting on the boxes? Is it the same tape?

I have never bought a unit moved by a moving company and was disappointed. Some people put a lot of faith in newly bought boxes, I do not. Look at the whole unit, not just bits and pieces. You are buying the whole unit so look for ways to cash in on every item. Everything can be sold unless it is broken **(some broken items like laptops do well on eBay)** it is a matter of pricing.

I have gotten more good stuff out of boxes people picked up behind a store than in new boxes. This is my theory, if they had time to gather boxes this was a planned move, planned moves means careful packing which is what you want. It doesn't matter how good something was if it was broken during the move. All areas of the country are different. Use this as a guide to formulate your own template or buying profile.

Speaking of boxes—count the boxes if you can, when you get to twenty five or more boxes in a self storage unit you are more than likely going to get something valuable. Are the boxes full? Do they sit heavy? **By this I mean, are they crushing the box below?** If they are stacked—say five high and there is not any pressure, meaning they are not crushing the box below to a degree, it is something very light in them.

Life is what you make it!

From my experience, light equals low value—not always but most of the time. If there is dust in the unit, has it been disturbed? Look for continuity in the unit. Do not be distracted by the chatter that is going on around you stay focused and work your plan. Note the condition of the furniture, scratches are not detrimental, but they will lower the value of your furniture significantly. This is where the spot light can make you money or save you money.

Working Your Light!

Learn to work your light; if there are a lot of people at the auction; hit the room with short bursts. You are not trying to help people bid against you using your own light! This will take practice. There was a term we used in the Army called "stick and move". Be active like a basketball player with your light. Folks will key in on you if you stay in one spot too long.

You can use this tactic as a red herring, take your light and shine it for an extended period of time on an area to lull people into thinking there is something there—some people will bid based on this alone, they think you know something.

If you see something interesting, go back to it when the crowd thins out (if there is a crowd).

Light Etiquette—this gets funny.

A lot of people, at the beginning of the auction, will talk about you and your "big" light. These same folks will turn around and ask to use it! I say no. I only let people I knew were not going to bid against me use it on other units. Just beware! I know you would hate it like a mug it someone beats you out of a unit using your own light!

Bird-dogging—using someone else's light to your advantage.

There will be a few folks who do not know how to work their light. You can shoulder surf these people all day! Just get right behind them and wait. Usually the folks with big mouths are the easiest pickings.

Check out the corners and the back of the unit if you can see it, if not ask the property manager how big the unit is. Sometimes the unit is stacked up so high you cannot tell how big it is. Bigger is better, more bang for your buck. If you cannot get a good read on the size of the unit, walk to a corner and look at the side of the building, after a while you can gauge unit size in a matter of seconds. Some units you will be able to see everything in it because it is either large or the items are spaced out all over the place. In this case, knowledge becomes your secret weapon.

I once stood next to guy saying a set of Powerblocks were worth only a couple of bucks. I got the PowerBlock and the stand that supports them, for ten dollars. I sold the set on eBay for $550. As you buy and research various items, over time your knowledge base will increase, making it easier for you to assess your units. You will become a virtual walking encyclopedia of pre–owned items. Knowledge, in terms of fast pricing and outlets to sale a particular item will serve you well in other areas of your life.

Storage auction unit assessment is part art and science. The science is derived from the marketplace; it does not matter how well the item looks or how great the item is if the marketplace will only bear a certain price. In the beginning of your storage auction buying career, there will be many things that you do not know the current price of or what the market will bear. This will be a fundamentally important part of your unit assessment task. When you are assessing a unit during the auction, time is working against you, unless the unit is a dog. No one moves a unit like that very fast, but pay attention on all units—junk can make you money.

Get on the floor or ground and use your light to check out the back of the unit, if you can. This is why I say wear old clothes. If you see multiple chair legs, more than likely it is a dining room set. Look for sofas, washer and dryers, read the writing on the boxes, if it is all the same, more than likely what is written on the box is in the box.

If the unit is pretty well stacked, neat and orderly there is some good stuff in there! Let us define the good stuff: anything that you can sell and make money. Many people are on a treasure hunt. There is nothing wrong with looking for the unique and special in a storage unit that comes up for auction. The problem rears its head when your expectations are set to only see these types of units as valuable. Everything that sold once, will sell again. It is just a matter of price and condition.

I did say this was intense!

Do not worry if you do not get all of this right the first time. Learning how to properly assess a unit, in a matter of seconds to a few minutes, is a skill set that will take you some time and practice to develop. Some auctions are long and drawn out but most are over within 90 seconds. That is why you want to get to the door as soon as possible.

One of my favorite tricks was to **"jump the bid"**. This is a method of mentally screwing with your competition. Jumping the bid is making a bid as soon as you see the unit. You have not even properly assessed the unit, but it is a unit that you like. **A parallel to this method would be when the offensive teams during a football game, calls a quick snap.**

Often, you will accomplish one of two things. You can get the unit cheaper than you normally would have bought it for because they're not paying attention. The second thing is you rush your competition into making quick decisions that may or may not be in their best interest. If your competition is working with a limited budget, and they make a quick decision and buy a unit that does not fit their requirements; they are reduced of capital and saddled with a unit that may be hard for them to sell.

This tactic served me well for many years, I would flush the capital of many people and buy several or better units at a reduced price later in the day. As my uncle J Rock would say "this is chess, not checkers muthersucker!" By watching your competition, which will be identified as anyone that is attending the auction, you will learn a lot about their habits and business practices. Do not just go to auctions, become a student of the game.

Life is what you make it!

Storage Auction Unit Profiling

Storage auction unit profiling, is researching the units before the auction occurs based on the tenant's name. Based on what you find will determine if you will attend the auction and after looking over the unit, decide to bid on it.

There are two ways to do this storage auction unit profiling. One depends on your knowledge base and the other depends on Google. Many people of note, fall on hard times or dire circumstances, just like the rest of us. Frequently, these people have exceptionally great stuff in the storage auction unit that they are about to lose. I depended upon my knowledge base.

Atlanta is a city full of people that became famous fast. Usually their fame and status, along with their money disappears faster than they came about. When the auction notices are placed in the newspaper, online classifieds and legal organs, many times you will have the full name of the person. If it is an unusual name, that makes it easy to research that person and qualify them as someone that you would want to chase their unit. If you guessed correctly and get the unit, it is a beautiful thing. There are some pitfalls to this method—it is time consuming. Many of those people that you have profiled will pay off their unit and it will not go up for auction. People with common names, it becomes **a needle in the haystack** type search.

For those of you who operate in a limited geographic area or they do not have that many auctions in your area, this would be the thing to do. If you're in an area similar to Atlanta, a city that has more auctions then you could ever attend; this could be a very challenging method of qualifying units to purchase. However, if you want to choose this route of unit qualification, you will want to invest in a smart phone with a very fast web browser. This way, you can do your research in the field, which will save you a lot of time and wasted effort.

In a backhanded way, I have gotten quite a few units because I knew who the person was by the auction announcement. This is another case of knowledge being power. At times I can be an information junkie, but I read the newspaper, local magazines and blog. This is a manner of learning who the people of note are in your city, without actually making it a priority. I will give you an example, I read an article about the producer that worked at CNN, and this person had a unique name. That persons unit came up for auction. During the auction, I kept questioning myself is this really the same person? I bid and won the unit and in fact it was that person and the unit was rich with CNN paraphernalia and some outstanding personal belongings and furniture. I bought this unit for $85.00 and sold everything in it, making $1600. So, yes storage auction unit profiling can work, if all of the conditions are right.

Don't Judge a Unit By Its Junk!

Yes, I know that is confusing! I will explain. When you're assessing a unit, you must look beyond what you see in the unit. What I mean by this is, if you see a chair that is broken and clearly not of use to anyone, you do not dismiss the unit because of that fact alone. Instead, you alter your thinking; you want to know if at all possible who made that chair!

This is the thing; many items are broken during the move that were perfectly serviceable before the move. The reason that you want to know the history or maker of that chair is because that information, may give you insight on the other items that are in excellent condition.

This is an example. I was at an auction and we arrived at this unit. As soon as the door went up, a busted chair fell out of the unit and we could see that many of the things at the door of the unit were damaged. This was an immediate turn off to most of the people in the auction crowd. Being the helpful soul that I am, I picked up the chair and placed it back in the unit. During my good deed of that day, I noticed on the bottom of the chair the word **"Baker"** and my heart begin to race. This maker of furniture only sells high-end, contemporary and traditional-styled furniture. One chair for the dining room set can run you $1600! To put that in the proper context, you can stop reading this book and go to our furniture store and buy a very nice dining room set with a China cabinet for less than the cost of that one **"Baker"** chair.

I let the crowd subside, 80% of the people walked off after they saw the busted furniture. A few people hung around, I looked at the manager and *said "I will give you $50.00 for this shit"* and kind of laughed saying I knew one of these other people would outbid me and at that juncture, I started to walk off. The manager looked at the others that remained; they shrugged their shoulders and clearly indicated they were not bidding. One of the other potential buyers *said* ***"Buddy, you are stuck with that one!"*** he laughed and walked off.

The manager wrote my name down and I placed my lock on the 10 x 30 unit in one of the wealthiest neighborhoods in Atlanta that I got for $50.00! After getting into the unit, I discovered the items in the first 5 feet of the unit were damaged. The other 25 feet of stuff was in awesome condition! When I sold everything, I cleared $5000!

The Best Unit I Ever Got!

The best unit that I ever bought was the one that was in Conyers, Georgia and it was a unit that looked like hell. I bought it for $1.00 and made over $62,000 within six months. Many of you reading this book would have never bought it. I want to emphatically urge you to look at the complete unit before making a decision to pass. This due diligence can put money in your pockets!

Many auction buyers pass on clothes; you can make a good income with clothes although it is a great deal of work. One of my eBay ID's was for used clothing only and we did quite well on that ID for many years. I got a lot of the clothing for free from other auction people who did not want to move them!

Very old stuff can be very good stuff, the possession of folks who have passed on or moved into a nursing home. This stuff often ends up in storage units; many people put their parents stuff in storage and lose it.

It is very sad that the possessions of many members from the group titled **"The Greatest Generation"** often have their lifelong possessions capriciously cast about, without love and respect. I learned early on the signs of what I call —**a nursing home unit**—you will see medical devices, oxygen tanks, wheel chairs, portable toilets, insulin needle boxes and sometimes prosthesis, usually a leg. It is clear that the former owner of the items that you are bidding on was in poor health.

The offspring of these people usually throw them in a home and sell the house of the elder person. If I had to guess, I would estimate 18% of the units that I bought fit this description. Many times the kids leave antique glass, books, medals, uniforms, and vintage clothing in the units. Check eBay and see what antique clothing or vintage clothing is going for to see what I mean. Vintage and antique clothing is super hot right now! If what you find is in excellent to great condition it may be worth more than gold, literally!

Older people are consistently better at maintaining the condition of the items that they have. There is a very good chance if you find something of value it will be in sellable condition. Another thing about these types of units is the elderly and people from that generation tend to be more sentimental than our generation. What this means for you is this can be a good thing or bad thing. They save everything!

These are the units that you'll find silver certificates, McCoy pottery, vintage Tiffany and Co., sterling silver flatware sets, pocket watches, beautiful antique and vintage jewelry. I routinely found items like these in those older people's units. You want to be on the lookout for this type of unit. Other characteristics of this type of unit will be the avocado and almond color appliances and old funky "I'm a pimp" type furniture. When you see red crushed velvet, be on high alert!

This is the point which you need to develop the **"eye"**. I cannot recall how many units that I bought and the most valuable item was right in front of everyone! Many storage auction buyers are seeking immediate gratification and items that fit whatever means immediate gratification in their eyes.

A good example of this was the unit that I bought with the butcher's block. The butcher's block was sitting right smack in the middle of the unit at the front door. There were other interesting things in the unit, but I bought the unit because something spoke to me that that hunk of wood would make me some money. In my mind, I was thinking $100; it sold for $500. Butcher blocks in great condition that are solid wood are hard to find.

People that collect those items will pay a good price and travel to pick it up. Do not be lulled into the immediate gratification trap. There are many wonderful and valuable items in the world and you cannot sell all of them within the hour to earn a ton of cash. Some of the items that you pull out of storage auction units will require research and placing in the proper sales channel.

Electronics & Appliances

Electronics are a great seller and you will come across many computers, Sony Play Stations, Xboxes, TV's, stereos, iPods, games, tons and tons of cell phones, just about any electronic item or toy that you can think of. We are in the age of the flat panel, LCD or plasma television sets. These are the most fragile electronic items to come out in a longtime. When you come across flat panel televisions, never stack anything on top of it and move it in the same position that you'll watch it. This means never put it on its side or top when moving it. Although the newer ones are not as fragile, be very careful until you get it home. It is better to be safe than mad that you just broke $200-$500 worth of merchandise.

All types of small appliances such as blenders, mixers and microwave ovens do very well used. What really sells well are high–end kitchen gadgets. I can never keep that stuff. It is very expensive, yet very desirable. People love fancy cooking stuff. From expensive pots and pans to ceramic chef knife sets, bright and colorful equates to a fast sale. Mixers do really well from September until May—I do not know why—but if I had a mixer during those months it lasted no longer than a few days.

When you buy the bigger units, there is a very good chance that you *will buy appliances.*

"Washer and dryer sets, window air conditioners, heaters, side by side refrigerators, stoves, dishwashers, hot water heaters, sinks and tubs and more. "

All of these items can be resold, you just need to test and ensure that they work. In fact, appliances sell well and fast. No one just buys a washer or a dryer; they need a washer and dryer set. When you buy the things that people need, the sale is easy when the price is right. Do not be afraid to sell appliances. There is one thing that you should know about appliances—refrigerators that do not work are very hard to dispose of—you just can't throw them away. The Freon must be removed by a certified technician before most landfills will accept the refrigerator, if they accept them at all.

A word about electronics—items left in a non-climate control unit tend to have issues if they have been there for a very long time. Strangely enough this does not impact those heavy and prehistoric TVs from the fifties, sixties seventies and eighties, those items work just fine! Always plug up your items you want to sell on eBay and let them run for a few days, just to make sure they are okay to be sold.

Office Furniture

In the early days I was the only one in Atlanta on the auction trail that knew the true value of office furniture in these units. I used to sell contract furniture which is the formal name for office furniture, cubicles and task chairs. In the beginning I was stealing these units for next to nothing!

Office furniture can be an excellent profit maker, if you have the space and labor to move it. I used to get office furniture units very cheap, until one of the regulars came into my shop and saw the prices that I had on the office furniture and people were buying it. He told everyone! That ended my delicious run of getting units that made me $2000–$4000 for $5.00 bids and $10.00 bids. Another note, try to keep other auction people out of your business; they can mess up a good thing!

Life is what you make it!

This is another item that you will find in office furniture units; it is the modular phone system. This would be the controller and or the phones. Office phones are entirely different animals, and no you cannot take them home and plug them into the wall. They operate on a closed system—phone systems can easily run a small company $5000–$150,000, and it depends on the size of the system and the complexity of the requirements of that company.

Server racks, these are the metal frames that hold the servers for the company's IT room. Many businesses use storage facilities as mini warehouses. I have bought several servers, server racks, computer equipment and audio visual equipment. Business units are the type of units that you will frequently see this type of hardware in. I will give you an example; those little projectors for presentations can be as cheap as $300 or as expensive as $10,000!

For many years I made a lot of money off of business storage auction units. The number one reason that this was the case was very few people were selling online back then and many had no idea how expensive commercial equipment can be. There is a healthy and vigorous market for used and current commercial computers, restaurant and medical equipment. Medical equipment can be a little tricky, some of those items you can only sell to medical facilities, by law! Trust me, it is worth the hassle!

As you begin to decipher what is in the unit, think of yourself as an archeologist looking over some bones. If they can tell how big an animal was and what it ate a million years ago, with less information than you are going to have when the door goes up, you can do this! For me this was the most fun; it is like solving a big puzzle with the payoff being cash!

Look for the shopping bags; are they from high end stores?

Are you looking at high grade furniture?

Name brand professional tools such as MAC or Snap-On are outrageously expensive and sell quite well in the secondary market.

You will see construction equipment, power washing services; yes the whole setup in a storage unit—even landscaping equipment, up for sale. Sometimes you will have the trailer and equipment in the lot.

If you go to enough auctions you will see several different types of businesses in self storage units. Some of the businesses you will find in a storage unit are, but not limited to, vending, HVAC, landscaping, plumbing,

Life is what you make it!

contractor, masonry, and electrical. Sales representatives keep their samples in storage units; T-Shirt vendors, shoe stores, eBay entrepreneurs, major online book sellers and engineering firms lose units also, and a lot of restaurant equipment. I have bought each of these types of units, many times over.

I know of people that started a side business for next to nothing with the items they bought at auction. Think of anything that you have in your house, anyone's house or a business—you will see in self storage auction unit. It is a high, to find a vintage Coco Chanel bracelet or a rare Roseville vase in your finds. If you buy a lot of storage units, you will come across these types of items. By a lot of units, I mean in the 20–40 per month range—that is 240–480 units a year; that is a lot of opportunity to hit it big!

Ahhhhhhhhhhhhhhhh..... You see a unit you want to bid on!

Learn How To Bid!

Bidding is an art, science and a lesson in diversion. Some people wink, tap, nod, kick, dip, touch their hat hold their finger in the air, yell yo! I knew one guy that would say "**UP! UP!**" Too increase his bid. As you can see, a lot goes on. This is by design to confuse you and to hide who is bidding; mainly to hide their bid from the other bidders—there is a lot of bad blood out there! So many people on the storage auction trail have it out for each other. I have personally seen people bid on units that they did not even want, because someone that they did not like was about to get a really good deal.

This is endemic of the storage auction lifestyle. Expect to piss people off, expect people to piss you off. When you're consciously running someone up that you have ill feelings towards and do not care if you make money or lose money on the unit, you officially have become a true storage auction buyer!

You got your eye on this unit, if you have summed it up correctly, you want to have a **winning bid of one third or less than what you can expect to make off of the unit.**

If you have to slide it to one half, alter that for ego or some very specialized knowledge has taken over. By this I mean, you know what the item or items in the unit are worth, and you can bid whatever and still come out on top.

The example of this would be a motorcycle frame. There are other items in the unit, and people are bidding on those items and the price is getting somewhat high. Without a doubt, you know that that frame is worth $1500 and the bidding is only around $350. Based on that one item alone, you can bid $500 and still more than triple your money. After dude snitched on my generous profit margins on office furniture, I paid what some considered to be very outrageous prices for office furniture units. I always made money on those units, and some of you reading this have that type of knowledge (about anything), you just don't know it yet!

Sometimes you are going purely on instinct and it can pay off. However, be careful with this—there is a thin line between instinct and adrenaline! Yes, it can be a rush to buy a unit...a big one! You have a number in your head, bid up to that number slowly, yes slowly. Start off low even if you know the unit is going to reach a thousand dollars or more, this is not a horse race, it is a marathon. Usually when the bidding slows, you are getting to the end, so the slow guy can win a lot of times by dragging it out!

Why?

Many of the auction hounds are compulsive and impulsive people; they get excited and yell out crazy bids to scare you off— or just bid wild. You stay calm and work your plan. By reading this book and preparing yourself to make, you will be light years ahead of them!

When the auctioneer says "**going once, going twice**"... **this is where you pop in your bid before he says sold!** Timing is critical on this and you need to be paying attention! This pisses people off and they lose focus! Instead of focusing on the unit, they are focusing on you! Which is great; many times they will stop bidding because they are tired of dealing with you! I cannot count how many units I got this way! The closest thing I can describe to this behavior is the art of trash talking while playing cards! There are some people who talk trash to make you lose focus—sometimes all it takes is a momentary lapse for the other guy to win—it is the same deal with the storage unit auctions!

This is a pitfall of bidding slow—it gives time to those who are not sure about the unit to make up their minds and start bidding. This can cost you more money. As you gain experience, you can learn to manage the auction—tell the auctioneer to close it, if others are taking too long to bid. I have actually pulled the door down and put my lock on the unit; this does not work all of the time. Unless you have a reputation of going after the people who run you up, running up another bidder will be defined as continuing to bid and you know you have no chance in hell of getting that unit. It is just a form of aggravation and entertainment.

There is an exception; running someone up can be part of an intimidation campaign. What I mean by this, say you're dealing with a whale **(a very big and consistent spender)**; you know cash to cash you will never win against this individual. However, if you consistently become a pain in his ass, then the game changes. Is it worth the money that he will lose by fighting you off each and every time, or is it better to let you have a few units so you'll run out of cash and leave him alone? The downside to this method is it could take a long period of time to wear down your opponent and you may find yourself paying far more for units than you really want to. This business tactic is not for the faint at heart or the thin of wallet, but it works!

One of the secondary benefits of this tactic is, other bidders will become intimidated by you. It is a David and Goliath type deal; they want to do the same thing, but they do not have the balls to do it. So when the whale is not around, you become the whale! On some guidelines to this tactic, only put this tactic into play on units you really want; you do not know when he will just say **"no mas"** which means the unit is now yours. I would not recommend this tactic for a newcomer, or someone with a very limited budget. This is just the toll that you pay if you choose to follow this road. This is a plan that you can follow later, when you have better capital and better cash flow. This method got me around a lot of people except for one and his ass retired years ago, thank God!

We all must crawl before we can walk—don't worry, there will be plenty of units in the future. The old heads, at some point, will retire or lose their passion for the business—just about all of the people who use to terrorize me are retired or scaled back so much they did not bother me at all my last few years in the business. Sometimes I would buy every unit to prove a point— you play with me, you go home empty handed. It is not fun to be out all day and you cannot buy one unit.

This is where knowing who you are dealing with comes in handy. Now if you are holding $10,000 or more in your pocket, go for what you know! There are not that many people on the auction trail that will be able to hang with you. Most people, after they spend $1000–$3000, are done for the day, week or month, until they sell some merchandise and recapitalized. Whether you're buying units or not, you can learn a phenomenal amount of information by being a regular attendee at storage auctions. If you're known as someone that shows up but never bids, they will become comfortable with you and start saying things around you that they should not! This is to your advantage. Regardless of how much money you have, you still have to buy the right units and within budget to track your money.

On sealed bid auctions or silent bid auctions, you write down your bid on a piece of paper. Now this is a totally different animal; you really have to assess the unit—but you are already performing that task. On sealed bids, many people grossly underbid or overbid.

This is how I did it. Once I put a price on the unit from my assessment—I usually added $45.00 up to $105, depending on how badly I wanted the unit—I have even gone as high as an additional $225. That was based more so on who was at the auction versus what was in the auction unit. On sealed bids, you never want your bid to end in an even number. As one of the old timers use to say "put a little change on it" which I did if I thought there was enough profit potential in the unit. In other words, you never want to bid in whole numbers on a silent bid—always throw in some change in your bid! Don't bid $110, bid $113.23, for example. People have won silent bids by 5¢ and then you become that guy who lost a unit because of a nickel! It is funny as hell!

Bidding is an art and you are going to have to practice it. Be calm even, and bid slowly; do not be in a hurry to spend money fast! If you see that you may need more time to clean out the unit, ask before the bidding is over—this is when you have the most leverage. Usually they will give you what you want within reason.

Bidding posture—make sure the auctioneer or manager can see you. I have seen folks lose good units by trying to bid cute with winks and nods. Once the guy or gal says sold, it is a done deal! No do over's. I know this sounds like a lot, but you can do it; it takes just a little time and practice! Trust me, if I could do it, you can do it!

Recap of what you do when bidding on a unit

Assess.

Assess again.

Come up with your high bid number, start as low as you can and work up.

Bid slowly and continue to assess unit while you bid.

If people are blocking the door nudge your way in!

Make sure you can be seen by the person conducting the auction.

Win your unit!

It takes practice, but it is well worth the effort!

8

Rut-Row!
Delinquent Renter at the Auction!

People who are losing their stuff sometimes come to the auction! It can be nothing, or they can lose it!

One sad part of this self storage auction business is that the person whose unit you are bidding on may be at the auction! Sometimes the whole family! Perhaps a friend of theirs is at the auction trying to win it back for them. This is on you and your business practices. Some will ask you not to bid on the unit, others will ask for the personal effects. I was a hard ass, if it was a good unit, I was bidding, if it was a crappy unit I left it alone.

I have seen many strange things happen when the delinquent tenant is allowed on the property. Many storage facility companies have a strict policy that once you are seriously late on your storage unit, you're denied access to the property unless you're coming to make a payment. I love people that run their storage facility like that, however many places do not have this policy and the poor unfortunate people get to watch bidders not only buy their possessions, but make discourteous comments on the things that they see in the unit. It's one thing to lose your shit; it is even more depressing to watch people talk like that about the things that you hold dear. A word of advice, you do not have to be a bleeding heart to understand this can be a heartbreaking moment for some of these people. As a rule, if I knew for certain that they were there, I kept my unkind comments to myself.

This is how you handle yourself if the delinquent tenant is on the property. Often, these people will try to discourage you from buying their unit. Some are humble and you can see it in their eyes that they're going through hell. Others are cocky, mean—a wide range of behavior from passive-aggressive, to outright begging. For very emotional people, this can be a very trying situation. I have seen people cry, scream and literally fall out in a fit on the pavement—kicking and screaming like a child. Be polite and firm, but stick to your plan. If you do not buy it, I guarantee you, someone else will. This is a point where you will make your own decision on how to conduct yourself in this type of situation. My rules were simple and they worked well for me. That may not be the case for you; with the economy being what it is, there is a very good chance that you will go to auction and see the people that are about to lose their life possessions, as a somber moment.

If they are there and you win their unit, which is now yours, close the door and lock the unit.

You can do it any way that you want, I just never liked dealing with the person whose unit I just bought; you never know their frame of mind. I have been insulted and propositioned, in relating to or dealing with someone that just lost their unit. Your main focus as a storage auction buyer is the profitability of your company. Yes, it is hard and it is cold, but that is life.

NEVER move the stuff with the folks whose unit you just bought still on the property. Come back later and get the stuff, **ASAP.** People break in units to reclaim their stuff; why they do not do this before the auction, is a mystery to me. Whatever you are going to give back to them let the property manager know about your intentions and leave it in the office; the less contact with the renter the better. They can come back later and get it.

Sometimes the storage company makes a mistake and sells a unit that they should not sell. This can be very interesting; it has happened to me eight times. Understand, this is not your problem and here are some steps to protect yourself. As long as you have paid for and have the receipt, it is your unit; however, if you have not moved the unit, it can get a little tricky! They can cut the lock and block your access; yes, they will give you your money back—sometimes in the form of a check! You paid cash and got a check back, now don't that just bite! Understand, this usually happens with the very nice units!

Why?

People with nice stuff are usually educated and educated people will sue in the wink of an eye! A suit can cost the storage company tens to hundreds of thousands of dollars!

Move the unit as soon as possible—the nicer the unit the faster you should move it! When they contact you, tell them you sold it already but you may be able to get it back—this way, if they really want it, they will meet your demands more quickly. Otherwise, they will pull the **"we really need your help on this one"** routine. Take one for the **gipper,** oh wait; you are not on their team, so why should you take the hit?

Ask the storage unit company for the estimated sale value of the unit. If you do give it back, there is a lot of work involved and it is a pain in the ass—you need to be compensated! Say you were going to make five thousand off the unit, ask for that and moving expenses—you are saving them a ton of money and they know it! They may play hardball, they may not, and your power lies in having the unit off of their premises. In this case, they need you more than you need them. Just some words to the wise: that is why I usually got my stuff off the lot as quickly as possible. It does not happen all of the time, but if you buy a lot of units, sooner or later it could happen to you. There is an element of risk to buying any storage unit, but after you get some experience this will be greatly minimized.

Think of it like going to Las Vegas and winning 80% to 90% of the time. **That is my view on risk—I can say out of twelve hundred plus units we bought over the years, there are eight that really stand out as stinkers, which I wished I had never bought! EIGHT!**

Yes, we hauled these beauties to the landfill and added more insult to injury by paying to throw it away! There were others that I only doubled my money, yes. That is bad when you have expenses and labor. For many this is a good unit! Why? Because they are not used to making money consistently! For most of the players in the storage auction

Life is what you make it!

business, it is a hobby and it is treated as such. Now, there is nothing wrong with that approach if you are doing it for fun and a little side money or off the books income. It is detrimental to your body, mind and wallet if you use that approach and you are attempting to make a living as a storage auction buyer.

You have got to have a plan; I do not think I can say that enough.

This is where having a game plan comes into play, you already know how you are going to move it, process it, where you are going to sell it, where to donate the items you can't sell and your online accounts are set up.

Most folks, when they begin, come out to buy a unit and then they come up with a game plan afterwards. I am one hundred percent serious. If you followed the steps outlined early in the book, you will have the space to store and process your merchandise and the feedback on your online accounts to make more money. That wastes a lot of precious time, not having a plan. Once you get into it you will see time as one of your most precious assets. Someone once told me "**scared money never made money**". If you are apprehensive, buy a few small units and work your way up. I would suggest getting the biggest unit you can with the money you have. More stuff equals more chances to hit a good lick. I know I have given you a lot of information to digest; once you have some units under your belt, you will be able to make these assessments in a matter of seconds or minutes.

Life is what you make it!

9

You Popped Your Cherry!

Shucky Darn! You just bought your first unit, ...awwwww

After months of reading, watching and prepping yourself for the business, the moment of truth is at hand. You just bought your first storage auction unit and you're so proud! You're actually in the unit, going through the boxes like a Tasmanian devil! Your unit is a hit, it looks good and you know you're going to make money. Now it's time to keep up the good work. It is time to take this puppy home and put the bowl on it. You, my friend, are about to experience a step that is just as crucial as buying the unit. What good is it to get a great storage auction unit if you do not load it and transport it correctly? Most of the damage that you see on the items in storage auction units happened during the move! This is what happens, when you use Heckle and Jeckle Moving Company!

Loading is just as crucial as buying!!!!

This next step is just as important as buying the unit— loading it correctly. Have you ever seen a guy going down the road with stuff in the back of the pickup truck or trailer blowing in the breeze? Yes, it looks crazy and something usually is broken by such sloppy moving or worse, it blows out of the back onto the highway! You never want to be this guy.

Now is when certain aspects of your game plan come in to play. If you have help or if you are doing it yourself, proper loading is just as important as proper buying. Most of these tips are common sense, but I have paid people only to watch that person attempt to put a heavy box of books on top of a box marked fragile. This was and is my biggest pet peeve, dollars going down the drain because of piss poor loading techniques!

I will keep it simple.

Bring out those old blankets, quilts or sheets and put some on the floor of the truck or trailer for the mattress set, if you have one or the sofa set. After assessing what you have, if you need to tie some sections of rope on the rails before you put anything in the truck; it is much easier that way.

Wrap up furniture and other items with nice finishes— you want to keep your new find in tip top shape; people want the best things in the world even at a garage sale! Sometimes your items will be already wrapped. You will acquire several moving blankets, hand trucks and dollies in this business. Take everything out of the unit if you can or leave room to work. The way that the items are pulled out of the unit may not be the best way to load your truck or trailer.

You want heavy and bulky at the head of the truck or on the bottom layer. Put mattresses on first and leave room to put the bed frames or mirror between the mattress and box spring if available. Load couches and love seats up on their ends, sometimes dressers. I usually never did it that way; I always stacked something on the dresser, but you will have more room that way. Be sure to put a blanket on the floor of your load vehicle to protect the furniture from damage.

Load your truck with the heavy items on the bottom and high as you can go with the lighter items, from the back of the cab to the end of the truck. Think Lego blocks—with the fragile Lego blocks on top, take the bags of clothes and use them as filler to keep the items from moving around. We usually moved items in a twenty four foot truck; modify as needed per your mode of transportation.

Trailers need to be balanced to prevent fish tailing, which is when the trailer swings side to side and yanks your truck along with it. It is a very scary thing; I did it once and had to pull over to rebalance the load. Same principle applies just make sure your trailer load is evenly distributed. One thing about loading yourself, if you do not work out, it would not be a bad time to start with a new workout routine. Cleaning out units is a lot of hard work, which is why we got people to load for us after a very short time. If you do it, pace yourself as you can be easily drained and have no energy left for marketing your new inventory. Each step is critical from finding the auctions, to loading your new inventory and of course selling the items for maximum profit.

Money Tip! You may be able to sell out of the unit. It all depends on what you have in there! Sometimes, it makes no sense to move it.

Life is what you make it!

I bought a unit full of scaffolds, lumber, plywood and drywall. This stuff is only good to someone in the construction trade or a DIY'er with a project. I took pictures and measured the items (this is important; when you sell online, measurements are mandatory!) I put it all online and sold the contents of the unit to three different people. They came with trailer and crews. **Bada Bing!**—it was gone and the only moving I did was during the picture session.

On your heavier items, on occasion you will come across items in a unit that you cannot move. Printing presses, pallets of brakes, heavy machinery, automobiles, tractors, these are some of the things that I have found in units that I bought. In the event that you get an item like this, there are several steps that you can use to help yourself out. The first tactic is to sell the item out of the unit, therefore you do not have to move it. Once you ascertain the value of the item, it may be in your best interest just to give the item away and move on. The person who is coming to pick it up will make the money but you no longer have to worry about the albatross that is hanging around your neck getting heavier each and every day. Storage facilities give you a very short period of time to clean out the units or they make you lease that unit.

Do your calculations and make a quick decision; some things are not worth hanging on to. In the case of automobiles, if you have a pickup truck you can rent a car hauler from UHAUL and move the car yourself. If the car is in park and there are no keys, there are two things that you can do:

1.) Weigh the cost of hiring a tow truck

2.) Renting the unit if you are going to scrap out the car

Scrapping out the car is taking it to your local metal recycling plant. You will have to remove the battery and take the gas tank off of the car before they will accept it. You will have to move it either way, just how quickly depends on which option you choose.

There are many solutions to moving heavy items out of a unit that you do not wish to sell. The quick rule is, if you can sell it and it is worth leaving in the unit until you sell it, rent the storage unit and work very hard at selling the item as quick as possible. Use all of your sales channels, friends, acquaintances and strangers. You will be amazed when you have something of value to offer, how likely you are to get rid of it when you approach people that you do not know. I got rid of a huge lot of bricks by approaching a very small woman who was driving a huge, monster pickup truck. It did not make sense to me that a woman that small would be driving such a huge truck, but as it turned out, her husband was a contractor. He and his crew came and picked up the bricks the same day. An open mouth gets fed.

One of the exciting parts of being an entrepreneur is you get to solve problems. Do not look as these challenges as a bad thing. They are points of growth and your range of experience increases with each challenge that you accomplish.

Trucks & Trailers

Ford F250

This is a great truck for hauling and used ones are just as good as the new ones. You want a V8 or Diesel engine if you will tow a trailer frequently. This truck can snatch a house down, if needed.

This is a NO! You cannot load much on it! If you already own one that is cool, but do not go out and buy one for this business.

Better! In this business, you will be hauling boxes and small items—you will need the rails for tie downs—this is a 10L x 6W

Best!

6ft X 12ft Tandem Axle Trailer

Perfect! Big Daddy! King of the road! 16 x 8

The high rails on the third trailer mean you can carry more stuff safely!   If you are going to move your items with a truck and a trailer, these are some examples of what you can buy and what not to buy! Remember, you will be moving many items, frequently; the more you can move on one trip the more time you will save! One major drawback to trailers is the weather. You can't move when it rains or if it rains in the middle of a move, you run the risk of damaged merchandise. That is why the 16 foot enclosed trailer is perfect; it gives you all the loading room of a 16 FT Box truck and the flexibility to leave it at home when you want to use your truck for some other task.

Trucks for the Serious Storage Auction Buyer

16 Ft Box Truck- easy to drive and not bad on gas, will move complete 10 x 10 units and smaller units, many people in the business have this truck. Used $3000-$10,000

16 Foot City Truck-same size box as the previous truck, but the major differences here are a diesel engine and maneuverability. Many older storage facilities are too small for larger trucks.

27 FT Straight Truck- my favorite! You can move a 10 x 25 in one trip in this bad boy! Not the best on petro! $6000-$25,000.

24 FT City Cab- The Ultimate!- the maneuverability of the smaller trucks and the load carry capacity of the big truck, loved it! $10,000-$50,000.00

Great All Round Load Vehicle! Sprinter Van

Holds as much as a 16 Foot Box Truck with excellent gas mileage.

I rented it several times and it is great for that mid level storage auction buyer. I put this information in the book to give you an idea of what is out there for you and what worked for me. If you are seeking to be a store owner—a high volume seller, you will need one or even two of the larger trucks. The time you save, by doing more per truck load, will show up in your balance sheet in black. I understand you are not going to go out there and buy a new vehicle; this is something to work towards. This information is to help you plan your steps for the future growth of your business.

Maintenance

Maintenance on the bigger trucks is a different ballgame. Oil changes on the diesels range in price from $150–$225 and they are required every 10,000 miles. On the diesel with the turbo charger, you do not want to be sloppy with your maintenance. Always perform the maintenance on your vehicle before the scheduled time or right on time. This vehicle takes care of you by making you money. You must return the favor. Usually, if the maintenance is performed as prescribed by the user manual, you will not have a lot of problems out of your truck. They were designed and built for heavy use.

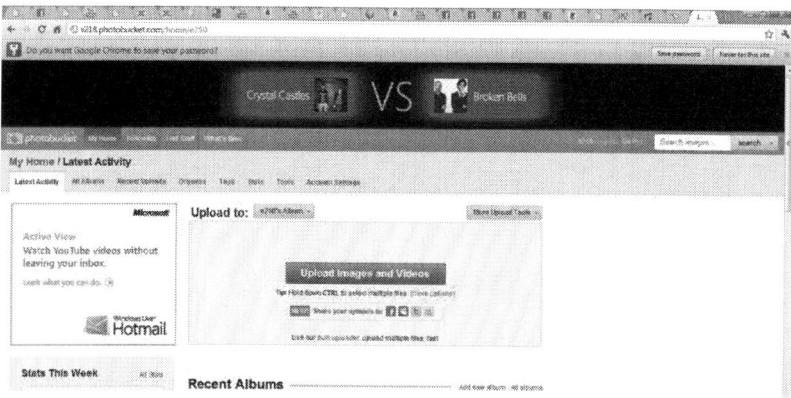

10

Open For Business

You have your first brand new and shiny unit and you are ready to sell the contents and make some money. When we

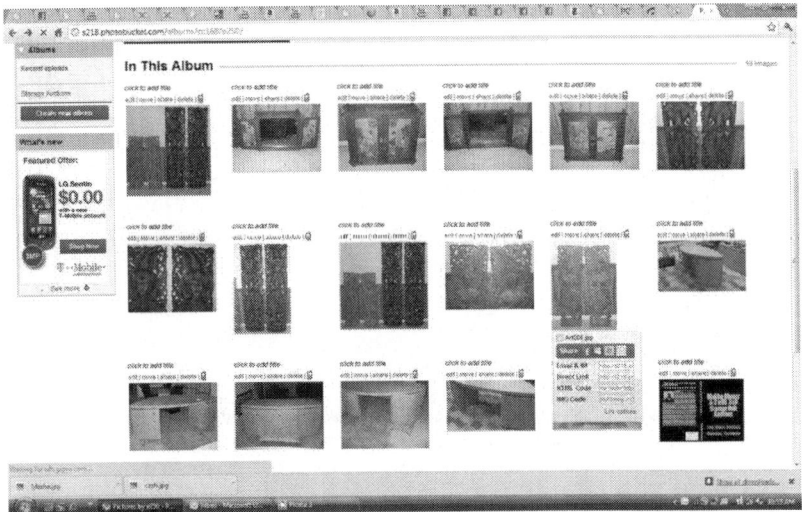

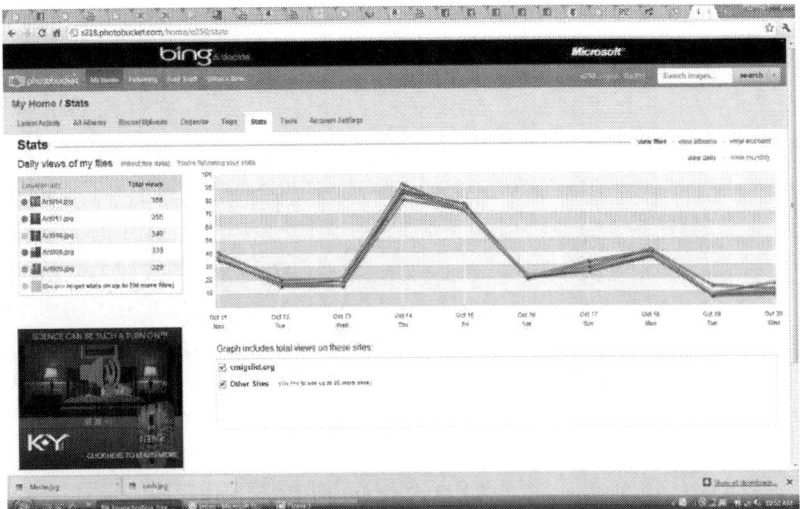

first started this journey, I gave you a set of tasks to perform; if you did that, the rest of this will be a snap! One of the things that made us successful was, we sold in all channels possible— consistently and in parallel! **This is mama's secret sauce.** Many people in the auction business conduct maximum profit triage on their units and throw the rest away. Just pulling out the obviously profitable items is a waste! You are essentially throwing

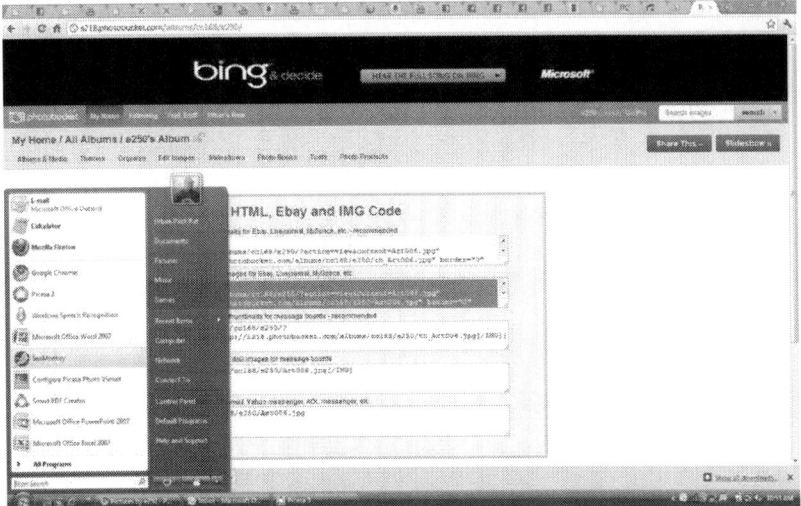

money away.   When putting up your eBay ads, include a customer service phone number and email address— remember the Google Voice account?   Use that number,

(Google voice) it gives you options and privacy—they can never find out who owns that number unless they go to Google corporate!

I found this out completely by accident; I wish I was that smart. One day my partner and I were discussing what we should put on eBay—she was saying name brand items and I was thinking antiques. Being a smart ass, I took one unit and put everything out of that unit up at a **99¢** opening bid. The unit was only $20 and I thought we could do perhaps a $100 on the stuff. There were one hundred items from the unit; items ranging from pots to silver jewelry. I took one

picture per item and wrote a short description, not too involved. Well, seven days later we had $760.00. Many

Life is what you make it!

items went for a dollar and several went for twenty to fifty dollars. But we sold every item!

Why?

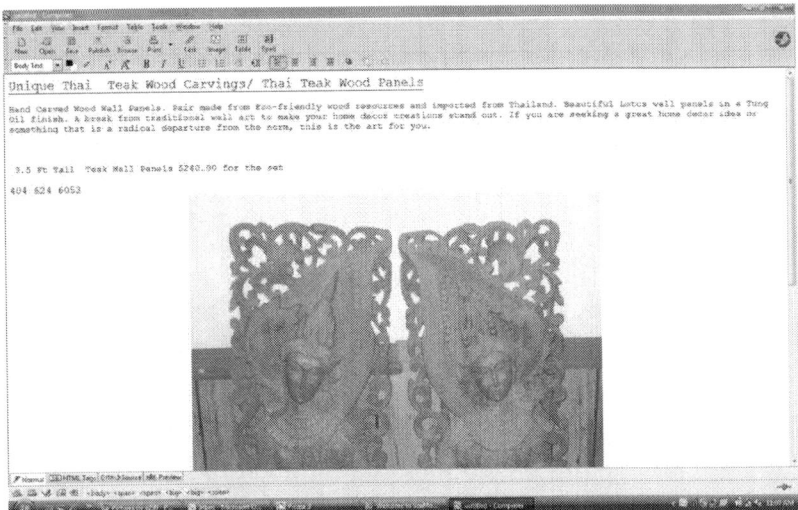

We had critical mass; many people bought two or more items to save on the shipping. We had cross pollination, I did not fully understand it, so I took another unit with four hundred items and put up fifty a day, same deal—one

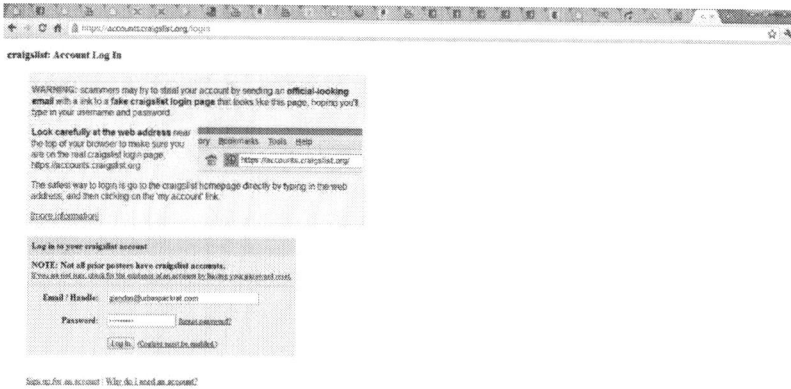

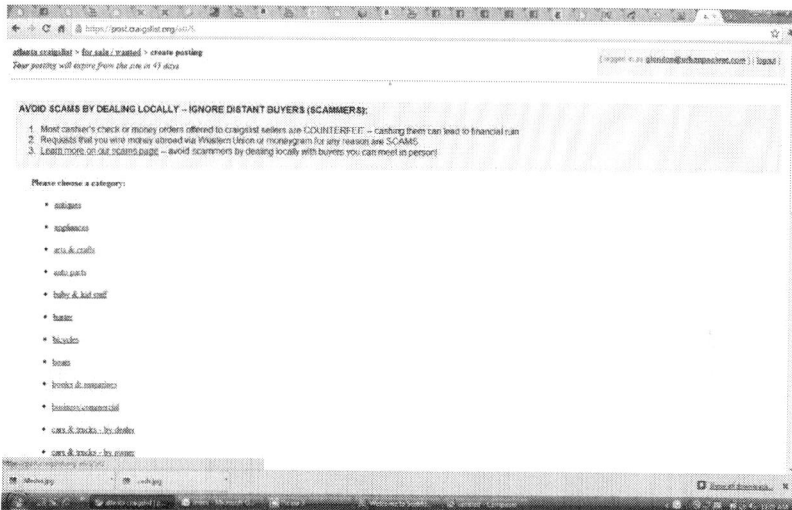

picture and a very short description, this unit cost us $200 dollars, I was taking a chance—so I thought...

Result? $1600!

I noticed we had people signing up for the newsletter. This is why I told you to start early with your eBay and PayPal accounts—if you follow this plan, you will hit their limits

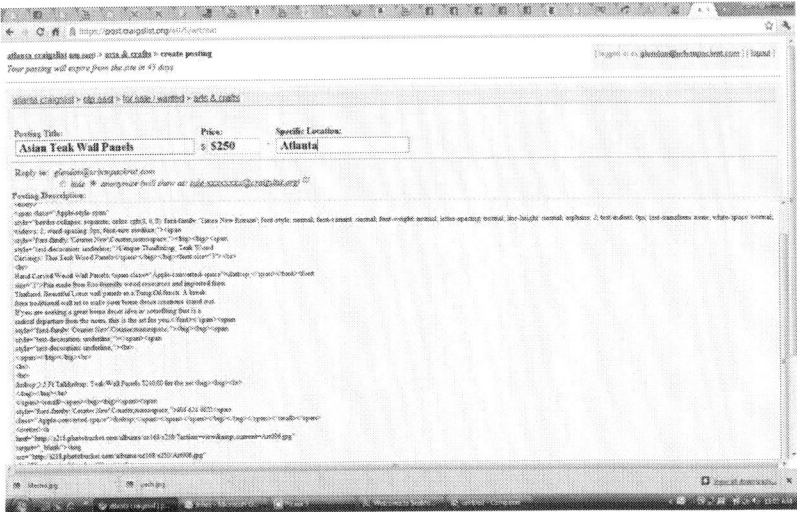

and PayPal alerts very quickly. We did and I went through a lot of crap to get my accounts reinstated. I did nothing wrong the reps told me, it just part of a ROUTINE check.

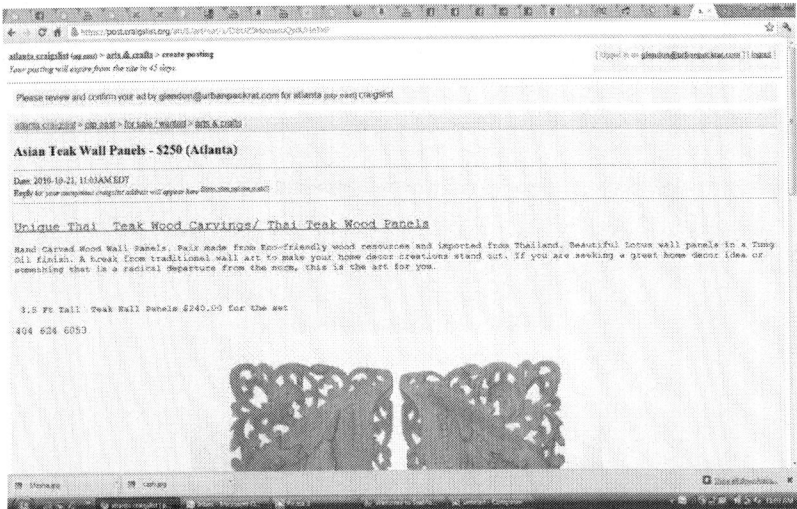

Why?

During the last seven years, people are making less profit on eBay. Notice I said profit. There are many people making a lot of money on eBay every day, but what is the

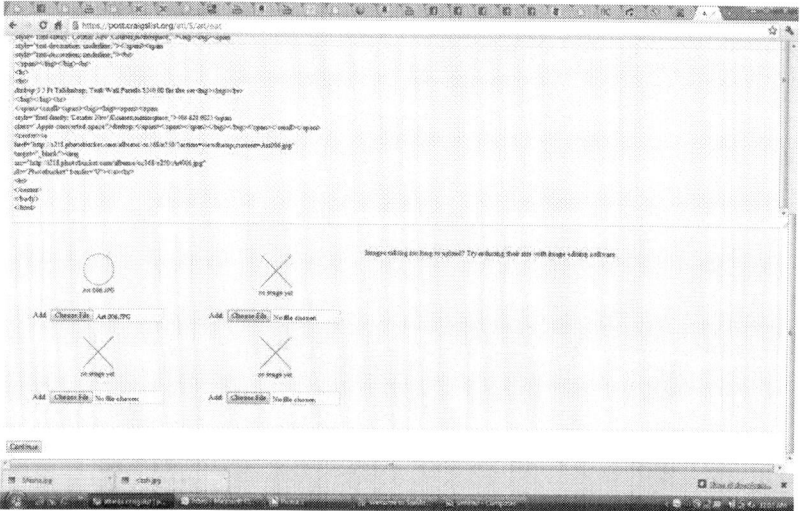

net on their sales? The net is the juicy part that goes into your pocket or into growing your business—the rest is expenses. It seems strange to eBay and PayPal that

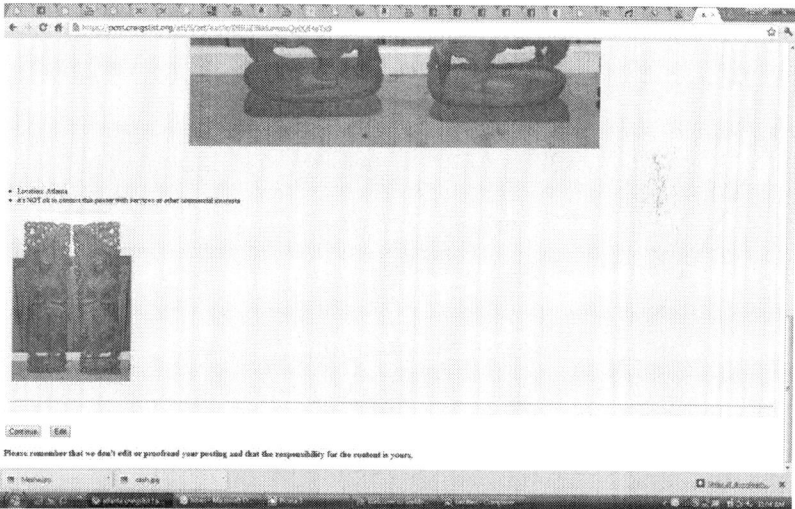

someone new is raking it in like that!   Some will say they are worrying about fraud, in some cases yes, in your case no. You are selling used, everyday items, for the most part.

Life is what you make it!

You are selling faster and making money quicker than normal and to eBay/PayPal (they might as well be the same company) this is not normal!

By getting your merchandise out of storage units and employing this strategy, you can move a lot of merchandise

quickly, thus making money quickly. We were getting seven

Life is what you make it!

hundred to eight hundred feedbacks per month and if you know anything about eBay, more than half of your bidders will not leave feedback! These feedbacks were the result of two thousand items per month being sold and we shipped merchandise seven days a week. This is the method we used to get there and you can too!

While you are on eBay, pay attention to the feedback numbers of other sellers and notice how MOST sellers are fewer than two thousand feedbacks; there is a reason. They are not selling that much stuff! Sure you are going to have someone with one hundred thousand feedbacks, however this is atypical, not the norm. Many people have been sold on the dream of eBay—that you have your own business and can run it anyway that you desire—this is not true, in fact it is a lie! There is a group of sellers on eBay that you can research today and see how my methods work.

Check out the feedback and the prices pawn shops get on their merchandise sold on eBay. Pawn shops sell a wide variety of merchandise and usually attract a larger number of bidders and regular customers—yes, regular customers shop online. I noticed this after I started putting everything up from the units on eBay. We had followers and requests for certain items. It is not going to be easy, that is why I suggest you start small and work your way up. Customer service will be the key to your success; you have to make sure your items are as described and you will avoid many hassles online.

Some of you will be blindsided by the fact that you can get more in person, totally missing the fact that you are not going to sell everything in a store, garage sale, or flea market. However, if it is cheap enough, you can virtually move everything on eBay! Furniture, appliances, yes, people will travel for a deal and no, you do not have to ship! It is constant money; imagine pulling $400 dollars out the ATM machine every day and transferring a lot to your checking account daily!

Whatever large items you have on eBay, run a parallel ad on Craigslist. By parallel, I mean the same words, same phone number and the same picture. Many people on Craigslist are lookers and will click on your ad, which is wonderful! This will get you indexed in Google within a matter of minutes to hours and it will make both your eBay and Craigslist items easier to find and ultimately sell. Once your item is sold take it down off eBay or Craigslist. Are you worrying about having the same item up in two places? DON'T! Many people wait until the last minute to bid, even if it is a buy it now! Once you get your PayPal account formatted (this means they are not limiting or holding back any of your sales) you can use the email payment invoice feature to accept credit cards for some of your Craigslist sales, if you so desire. I found this very useful on Craigslist, often folks will not have the cash, but they do have that amount on their credit card.

There have been many changes to eBay since we started this. I would now advise starting auctions items off at 2.99 or 3.99 or buy it now pricing with the lowest price you will accept and make sure your shipping is lower than others—high shipping can turn buyers off—even when with the shipping, the item is still significantly cheaper than new. This is strange, but true! Customer behavior online is very much like customer behavior in store settings, except they can price shop in seconds versus all day driving around town!

A Word About eBay

eBay is not your business, I alluded to this earlier. As we walk down this path of e-commerce, know that eBay is not your business. **You are, for all practical purposes, just an independent contractor that does not get a 1099.** Why is this important? It is crazy important! When you go into this world of eBay, thinking it is your business, you are going to get your feelings hurt! You do not dictate policy or even determine when and how you are paid! (if you are new). There are many things that eBay does that impacts you and your bottom line. Yes, it sucks royally; now that you know what the real deal is though, you can govern yourself according. Knowing the rules of engagement can make all of the difference in the world to your mental and financial health. Now to the good part, bar none eBay is the best portal for moving pre-owned merchandise on the planet thus far. With the right approach, you can make a lot of money. Do not get bogged down in **Powerseller** status and woe is the world stuff on eBay. You can do well and not lose your sanity. The first way to handle this is to set clear and high goals to accomplish. Know where you want to go with your business. Yes, your business. I can tell you how to make money on eBay and off eBay using eBay to get your customers! See, I told you there is some good stuff in here.

Once I realized what was going on with eBay, I made some serious changes. If you are not careful, the fees eBay set can eat you alive. There are several different routes to Rome and it is the same with your business! While you are at it, you can put that item in every free classified online and in your town. **Are you thinking of opening an eBay store?**

Read the words coming out of my mouth!

DO NOT OPEN AN eBAY STORE—IT IS A WASTE OF TIME, EFFORT AND MONEY!!!!!!!

Did you hear me? If not.......

DO NOT OPEN AN eBAY STORE—IT IS A WASTE OF TIME, EFFORT AND MONEY

!!!!!!!!!!!!!!!

Instead do this! After a few months, (some of you will be ready from day one) you will be ready to open up your own website; if you have the time, you can do it now. It is easy and there are several tools out there for you to use. You can even hook it up to your PayPal account! Once you get your domain name, change your eBay email address to one with that domain address and post it in all of your ads as your customer service email address, many potential bidders will go to your site to check it out—there you will have a site full of higher priced items that you do not have to pay eBay a dime for the referral! Forward that email address in your control panel to your Gmail address. I love Gmail, it gives you so many options and you can find emails faster with the search function.

Pimping Amazon

Put all media, CD's, DVD's and books on **major online book seller.** Over time, you will build a huge inventory. These items are good sellers at flea markets, garage sales and thrift stores. But guess what? You are not going to sell all of them and you are not going to get top dollar for these items. Yet on **Amazon,** someone will pay you $9 for one CD! In a resale setting you would be lucky to get a dollar or two for the same item.

If you buy enough units you will develop a serious major online book seller inventory! Once a week, pull out the cheaper stuff to make room for your better inventory that you will be getting frequently. Now we are rolling, once you get your initial inventory online, within two weeks you will start generating money every day! This is the fun part— getting paid frequently.

There were many storage auction regulars that only did the flea markets and nothing else. If it rained they were screwed; if it was too hot, they were screwed; if it was too cold they were screwed. Don't be that guy! I just prefer making money every day of the week. Now this is a suggestion. I had a store, eBay, Craigslist, major online book seller, the flea market and regular customers which was five sales channels. If you replicate my methods AND add the website to your arsenal you will have six sales channels. Think of six horses pulling a cart for you! A cart of cash! We had a new furniture website, which I maintained that was enough of a website to run, with SEO and other metrics to follow!

Going forward, in this economy, the more streams of income you have, the better. Once you get a feel for how you want to set up your business, then you can employ all of the methods or just a few. I know people who do sell only on major online book seller sites and they have a six figure income. It can be done! Storage unit auctions give you a unique position in the online sales world. You will be able to cross pollinate and sell a large variety of items. The advantages are many—with used items, you get the excitement of a one off deal and it keeps things fresh. Every month or week, if you buy a lot of units you will unearth tons of treasures. One benefit that I did not count on was the learning curve. After you have been in the business for a few years, you will have this database in your mind of the unique and special. I have learned so much that it boggles my mind. One example is the difference that a fine set of cookware makes in the preparation of your meals. I used to think people were out of their minds to pay hundreds to thousands of dollars for cookware. That is until I kept some pots for myself and wow! It does make a huge difference from preparation to cleanup. My cheap ass would have never known about the world of **Le Creuset** cook ware if it was not for a storage unit full of the stuff.

ebay, major online book seller and Craigslist

I have a love–hate relationship with eBay but it is necessary in this business to sell certain items quickly and for maximum profit. Of course you can sell your items in other venues; however, for the speed eBay provides, it is pretty hard to beat. **I LOVE CRAIGSLIST,** 'nuff said. To be successful on eBay, Major Online Book Seller and Craigslist is not hard. It is all a matter of inventory, great pictures and accurate descriptions.

Depending upon what level you want to start out with your business, I suggest paying for the **Photobucket.com** premium services. With this feature, you can track your hits on Craigslist. There are some other applications out there to do this but I like Photobucket because it is hidden and will not be removed or disabled by Craigslist bots. If you have never sold anything online before, lets keep it simple. The first thing you want to do is inventory triage. By this I mean look up all of the items you have for sale to see if they are **ebayable (any item that will fetch you at least $25 profit for low volume sellers or $3–$5 of profit for high volume sellers).** In the beginning, this will be very time consuming—going forward, you will become faster and many items you will not have to look up. You will develop the **"eye"** for eBay items. I will give you an example. I once had some pot handles, somewhat old and unusual looking. Well they had the name **Saladmaster** on the bottom of the handles and we got $42 for the pot holder's four pieces of plastic that cost $3.40 to mail. This taught me that anything can be worth something but until you look it up, you will not know what the value may be. The odd items do well on eBay. This is up to you on what you want to put up—I say put up all name brand items and let them roll. This will build feedback, experience and most importantly put cash in your pocket on a regular basis.

You can list using the eBay lister which is very time consuming and pricey with add–on options if you use them. When listing only a few items, it is not that bad to use. However, if you are putting up thirty items or more per day, then it will make sense to subscribe to an auction management platform such as **Inkfrog.com** (the simplest) to **ChannelAdvisor.com** (very robust and can be somewhat complex). I would suggest spending some time on **Auctionbytes.com.** It is a great resource site for eBay sellers and they stay on top of the changes in the online marketplace.

You have to spend some time evaluating what works for you. Most of these services offer a free trial, which is a great way to get your feet wet and learn more about auctions. It can be an exciting and profitable world. Remember, having fun makes life smoother, richer and less stressful. Okay, you did your inventory triage; you got a list of items to put up, now for the fun part! Taking pictures, there is a method for doing this also. On low margin items, take one very good picture and let it roll. There is no reason to spend a lot of time on pictures of items that you will only collect a few dollars on.

I like to do my tasks in groups; it creates flow and a sense of completion versus having a list of unfinished action items.

Examples of things not to take a lot of pictures of—clothing, unless you got someone to model the clothes which will increase sales, it is worth the effort but you have got to have the model. Read that as a hot guy or a sexy chick, it works well! One good clean shot and the description is all that is required. Use good judgment on this if you get a mink coat you will want to take a lot of shots, it is well worth the additional pain, the last fur I sold on eBay was somewhat ratty and it went for $380 but I had great pictures! Larger items, furniture, cars, certain toys collectibles— take many pictures of the item and spend the time with the description. Note, do not try and sell clothing on Craigslist unless you have a store. You will get a response, but it is not worth the effort required.

eBay is great for used clothing—you do have to measure the clothing which can slow you down a lot, it is something to think about. If you have the time, you can make $3000–$4000 or more a month selling nothing but used clothing— thus it can be worth the effort. It is a matter of do you want to deal with clothing which can be a pain in the ass. People are very picky when it comes to clothing, so you have been warned! My methods are about speed and efficiency.

Remember those tests you took in school? Finish the easy ones first, then go back and do the harder ones— the same principle will apply here. If you have never sold anything on eBay, then you should sit down and go through all of the tutorials about listing and selling. There are certain items that are banned, (guns, ammo, and fireworks) but you can sell tools for guns, parts for guns, just not the guns. This is rather insane when you think about it. I am not going to go into a deep and heavy discussion about eBay, it is too easy! The issue with eBay is the inventory. If you have the right inventory, you will have the sales. Years ago I was in the Merchandise Mart at a furniture show; there was this banner which changed my selling philosophy.

"Find out what people want and then buy it to sell to them "

Sounds simple, but it is not. That is why you see so much useless crap on the shelves of stores. My take on this is do not get caught up in gimmicks or overly involved in trying to make your ads on eBay and Craigslist too pretty. With the right stuff, you do not need those tactics.

The basics will serve you well:

Determine if your item is worth putting on eBay.

Research your item on eBay and price it to the market value —

NOT WHAT YOU THINK IT IS WORTH!

Post email address/phone number in the ads.

Clear pictures nice and crisp (go outside in the sunlight for jewelry and metal items)

Short accurate descriptions-many people online do not read the entire add, so it is pointless.

Cheap shipping this can make you or break you!

Use shorter auctions to get paid faster, 3 or 5 day auctions to increase cash flow.

Pack it well, ship it fast!

Life is what you make it!

Over communicate with your buyer.

Call all large bidders and thank them—my threshold was one thousand dollars. This is guaranteed feedback!

Ask for feedback, some think this is a bad idea but with more than half of your buyers not leaving feedback I think it a bad idea not to ask for feedback!

There is a lot of talk about the ad layout and colors for themes. None of that stuff matters when people are shopping on price! I am not saying a clean and concise layout doesn't help, because it does. However, do not let this drive your selling philosophy; make it a product–based selling method. With the right products, sales are easy! Keep your ads simple and to the point. I do advocate making sure that you have crisp and clear pictures. Perfect practice makes perfect pictures! If you are not using an auction management software life inkfrog.com, adding extra pictures to your eBay listing will cost you money using the eBay listing tool.

One free way to get as many free pictures in your ads is to use Photobucket.com. To keep it professional, you will need an HTML editor to make your ads more functional. For placement of pictures, font changes, font colors, etc., check out Sea Monkey, it is free!

http://www.seamonkey-project.org/

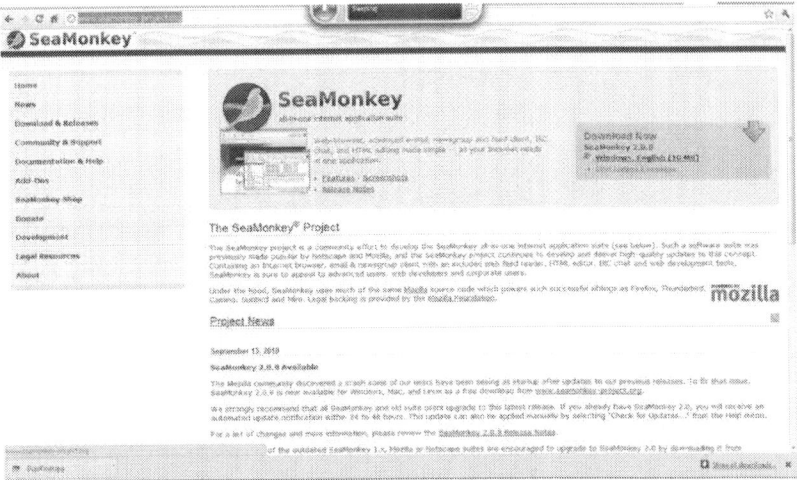

You can get by without the HTML editor in a pinch. But they are easy to use and will help you make money, so why not? One thing with eBay, if you are a new seller, expect to be monitored; even if you are a seasoned vet, if you change your selling habits, you will be treated like a new seller. They may limit the number of items you can sell in a specific time period. PayPal will hold your money, until the buyer receives the item or you can prove that the item was delivered. This will have a serious impact on cash flow, which means you will need to have money above and beyond your auction budget for shipping. Just something to remember as you fully develop your business plan. Knowing beforehand gives you plenty of time to prepare yourself for what may come.

Major Online Book Seller is so easy it does not need a lengthy explanation. Since you are putting up items from the storage unit auctions, it is like cake money. We really never put a lot of effort into it and it was usually $1800-$3600 a month. You just have to get rid of all of the penny stuff weekly or it will take over! If you are buying a lot, you can expect several hundred pieces of media a month if not over a thousand pieces. The only drawback is you must have money to ship the item and it takes two–four days for the money from Major Online Book Seller to make it to your checking account.

The eBay primer—a more in depth section on eBay!

I am going to get you to the point where you are in the "black" with your eBay business. At this point, you are making money not just generating revenue. HUGE, HUGE, HUGE, DIFFERENCE BETWEEN THE TWO!!! To do this, you will need the right mix of products and techniques. eBay changes rapidly which will just make you a better business person for life! Call eBay the basic training of business, if you do well here you can do well in other businesses!

I learned my business strategy when I was in the furniture business. One of my distributors was holding back a very nice furniture line for one dealer in town (they actually had a contractual agreement) which pissed me off to the highest level of pissitivity! They were charging crazy margins on this furniture line and I could not get a piece of the action. So being the kind of guy that I am, I convinced another manufacturer to make it and I sold the furniture at a price that the other guys could not match—let's just say my name is mud with that group. (Well, I did take pictures of the furniture in their showroom). Sometimes the only thing locking you out of the deal is your level of thinking. They would not let me play so I got my own playground! With a new set of see-saws!

In a word, the Black Ops strategy is, taking your business to the next level while looking through a different prism. I am all for you being happy and making money on eBay. If you do things the same way that everyone does it, you will yield the same results! Which have not been pretty. Over the last three years, many sellers bolted because it became untenable to make money on eBay. This is the most important aspect of your eBay process; with the right products, sales are way easy. Many people want to specialize and that is good, however you are going to severely impair your income unless you are doing high end items that sell quickly. It is going to be very frustrating and time consuming becoming a specialist. It can also be seasonal—what are you going to do when that season ends?

Here is a thought, go ahead and specialize, but also have a **SHOTGUN ID**. The SHOTGUN ID will be your source of consistent cash flow.

Most sellers on eBay who are making decent to very good income, have more than one eBay user ID. You can have as many as you want, just make sure they never interact with each other (i.e., you never bid on your own stuff). Each ID must have its own email address and that is it. This will allow you to be a niche player and also make more income. Create a game plan and make your user ID generic, that way you can sell anything and not have to go through identity crisis issues when you add a new product mix. Some people who believe in branding will shake their heads. To those folks I say this— go on eBay and check out as many user ID's as you want, research what these sellers have sold and 90% of the sellers on eBay are not selling over one hundred items per month!

This book is about making money, not some contrived brand that looks good but leaves your pockets flat. Now, there are many ways that you can find products to sell on eBay. The first place is your home. Go around your house and gather anything you do not want and make piles titled *"sellable, donate and I do not know"*. Do not limit yourself to small things— I have sold several large items on eBay and it is easy when you know how to do it! Okay we got the piles, get your computer and start researching what these items you have are going for on eBay—if anything. Once you fleshed out the easy stuff, things you know that are selling on eBay by your research, put them to the side for listing later. Now, for the items that did not make the first cut, there may be a way to sell them on eBay. It all depends on what you have. Here are some examples. No-name or mid-tier brand clothing— you can sell it on eBay, but not piece by piece; it is not worth the effort. However, if you got twenty, forty pieces of clothing or more in a lot, which is an attractive buy to a flea market person or a mother with a lot of kids. You can ship up to fifty pounds via FedEx for under $30.00 **(check on the website before you set it up, rates change)**.

People who are searching on eBay, look via name-brand, hence the reason name brand clothing does so well. But you have a lot of business owners looking for items to sell; they are looking for deals. Anything can be sold— it is a matter of price! Other items that do well are old knives, coins, weird things from other countries, your parents stuff, old books, prints that are by a well known artist, kooky stuff like pot handles, old fountain pens— the list is huge. You've got to wrap your mind around becoming a rapid researcher. That is the life blood of your eBay business.

To keep this section from becoming one hundred pages, you can just about sell anything on eBay from cars to services. Great sources of eBay items are people you know. Call up everyone you know and *say "I am looking to make some extra cash on eBay and I will take anything you do not want."* You will be surprised at how much clutter people have in their homes and how they will love for you to come and take it off their hands! Most people do not want to have a garage sale they would rather go shopping. On this move, there will be hard work, but with hard work comes opportunity.

In the Garage Sales Section of www.craigslist.org email folks early in the week, ask what they have and say you will take it all, (If you can handle it). Some will go for it, some will not but it is worth a shot! You need a lot of stuff to make money on eBay. Of course you will hit a grand slam but that is not going to be every day. We are shooting for consistent cash flow, which will give you money to save, live on, buy more stuff and pay your fees. You want to be in the area of 50–100 sales per week on eBay. With an average profit margin of $10.25 per item, that is $512–$1024.00 per week of your money! I break it down like that for this reason. Far too many people are looking at the gross sales numbers which, on eBay, are highly misleading. Say your sales are $7500.00 per month. (Buying new stuff).

Once you take out the cost of the product, fees, PayPal and refunds, you may be at a $1250.00 profit, **(this changes drastically with used items thrown in the product mix)** which, if you are currently doing eBay you could make more working at a job with less effort. There is also another problem with margins this low. When problems happen (and they will) you do not have enough capital to make things right for your customers without taking a bath. A mistake can literally wipe out your profit margin. I have been there! You want to obtain your inventory for the cheapest price possible.

I shied away from new items—too much upfront money and I did not know when the item would sell. However, I want to fully qualify that statement. I got my entire inventory out of storage units, so I never had to look anywhere else for eBay inventory. We sold thousands of items on eBay from furniture to diamonds, all out of the storage units. Finding items is really about using your imagination. This is another tactic I used to find items. Go to the furniture section of www.craigslist.org and go two or three weeks back and email the folks (all of them) "if you still have the furniture, I will take it off your hands". I got so much free stuff this way it will boggle your mind. Be of service to others and they will bless you! I know this may sound strange but, sometimes the difference between making it and not making it is asking for you want directly. They can only say no!

A Quick Rundown on Finding Items for eBay

Free Sources–everything is profit:

* Your home

* Your co workers

* Your friends—ask for the things they do not want

* Your family–same thing

* Drive through wealthy neighborhoods—it is amazing what they leave on the streets!

* Free section of www.craigslist.org

* Garage Sale section of www.craigslist.org —ask for the full deal help them out and they will help you out—I will take everything if you will give it to me.

* Ask strangers for stuff they do not want.

* Dumpster diving—yes, I did it! Got a Dell!

* The older ads on www.craigslist.org —go back a few weeks you will be surprised how many folks still have the item(s).

* Barter whatever service or skill you have for items—
(I got $950.00 worth of books at a garage sale for moving 5 things for free! Yes they were heavy!)

* Storage facilities— go by and leave your number; people leave stuff on the property of these businesses all of the time. Inform them that you will come get it!

You got to pay to play!

* Storage Auction Units- hard to beat!

* Garage Sales—some people have to make money

Life is what you make it!

* Estate Sales

* Liquidation Auctions

* Clearance Rack section

* Consignment Store Sales!

* Store closing liquidations

* Flea Markets

* Start a Foreclosure clean out business

* Thrift stores

Items that do well on eBay-This is a list of items that sold well on eBay for us. By no stretch of the imagination does this cover everything that does well but it is a start. We sold this stuff over and over.

Antiques

Apple Products—all

Apparel—new and used

Appliances—new and used

Bikes—used high end bikes do very well.

Broken Laptops

Camping Equipment

Collectibles

Comic Books—they have got to be rare!

Computers

Computer accessories

CD's—Lots

DVD's—Lots

Furniture—new and used

Shoes

Sporting Goods

Pictures, Pictures, Pictures

The quality of your pictures will make you or break you on eBay. I have seen so many people take jacked up pictures and want to make serious money when they were not serious in presenting the item. I believe pictures are more important than descriptions. **Unless you are dealing with a new item or a common item, one picture will suffice.**

I bought a unit at auction that contained the inventory of the Atlanta Beat Soccer Team. I sold 80% of that unit on eBay and each item was very unique. One item was a two story inflatable soccer cage. I blew it up (that was trip) and took about 15-20 pictures of it up and put it on eBay with a one word description and a few sentences about the condition. The feedback was 33, I think, and at the time it went for $380.00. The unit cost me $75.00. There was also a big inflatable letter "A" in the unit —only got $120.00 for it. Same deal, lots of pictures and a short description. On used items, very good to excellent pictures are your way to quick and profitable sales.

How to take great pictures

This is what worked for me. Find a backdrop for your studio, (does not have to be fancy) you can put a sign with your user ID, (I did not do the sign thing— I have seen it and it does make you stand out). I did kinda allow other things to creep in the pictures —say like a washer and dryer set I was selling in the warehouse— a lady bought it when she came to pick up her eBay winning. This is the Black Opt stuff, it looked a little tacky but I made money off of it. How are they going to buy it if they do not know you have it? Get a good camera—essential! Take several shots from different aspects of the item you are selling if it is unique; if it is a regular item and you do not expect to make a lot of money off of it, keep the pictures simple yet very clear. Use Google Picasca to put text on your pictures which makes it hard to steal them (yes, my pictures were so good that they were often stolen!) Take pictures of any damage and make those shots first in the eBay listing—this makes you appear to be straight forward and it builds trust and credibility rapidly. If you can, take your pictures outside— you get great shots on sunny days. If you sell jewelry or you want to sell jewelry, unless you have **a cloud dome,** taking pictures outside or in a very well sun-lit room will create some awesome images for your listing. Pictures that pop make people pause, the longer they stay, the greater chance that they will buy.

The Craigslist Photobucket Picture Pimp

I have referenced this technique over and over; however, many people continue to be confused. So, I have laid out in chronological order, my picture enhanced process.

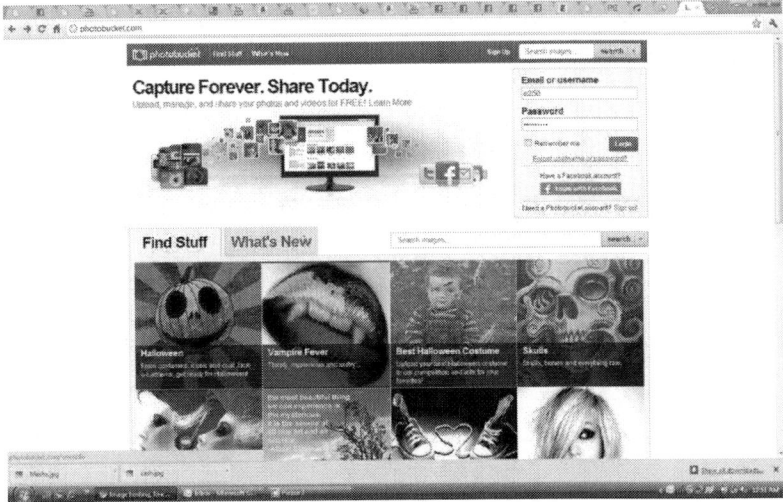

If you do not have a Photobucket account, it is quick and easy to sign up for one. To take full advantage of the all of the features offered, you will need to pay the very reasonable yearly or monthly fee.

This is my Photobucket account that I have had for years. Note the graph in the lower left hand corner. That is a powerful feature.

This is what it looks like when you open it. Photobucket gives you the ability to count your traffic on Craigslist. Google Analytics, it is not, but you will gleam very important information nonetheless. Once you know how many hits you are receiving, you can use this information to make changes to your ad If you are receiving many hits and no phone calls, it means that your price is too high for the marketplace.

I will use the image with the drop down menu to show you how to pimp your pictures on Craigslist.

Life is what you make it!

You will select the image by checking the box that appears when you hover over the picture, once this is done, move to the bottom of the page and select-Generate **HTML and IMG code button.**

You will be directed to the screen below, click on the type of images that you want to use, then copy the code.

If you already have SeaMonkey installed, open it. Your next step is to open the **composer** window—this is where you will create your Craigslist ad. This will open a blank form.

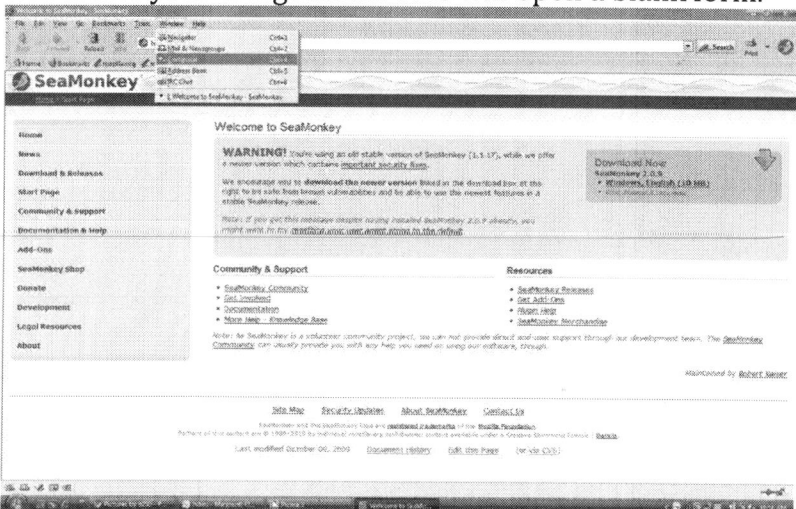

Move to the bottom of the window and select<HTML> source.

Open it and highlight the HTML formatting, which will already be there, I clean it out before I created an ad, to keep my work clean. Select the Normal button to arrive at the main window again

You will want to write the text aspect of your item first before pasting the image code in the ad

Life is what you make it!

Once that is done, you will go back to the <HTML> source button and open that window, this is when you will paste the image code into your ad. Select Normal.

This is the finished product! Go back to the <HTML> source button.

Copy your ad's HTML coding then Sign into your Craigslist account.

Select the category that you will list your item in. This is an art piece, so I will post it there.

Hit the **Post** link which will be in the upper right hand corner. Create your ad title, ad price and your location.

Paste the HTML code from your clipboard into the body of the posting form, add an image also, many people search image thumbnails before opening an ad.

Click the **Continue** button and you are almost done!

Review your ad and confirm it by entering the CAPTCHA™ into the confirmation /validation window, hit the Continue button, if you entered the CAPTCHA™ correctly you are done and you ad is posted on the Craigslist site! Your images will be eye catching! Note the differences in size and detail on the image Craigslist system allows you to display and your **"pimped"** image!

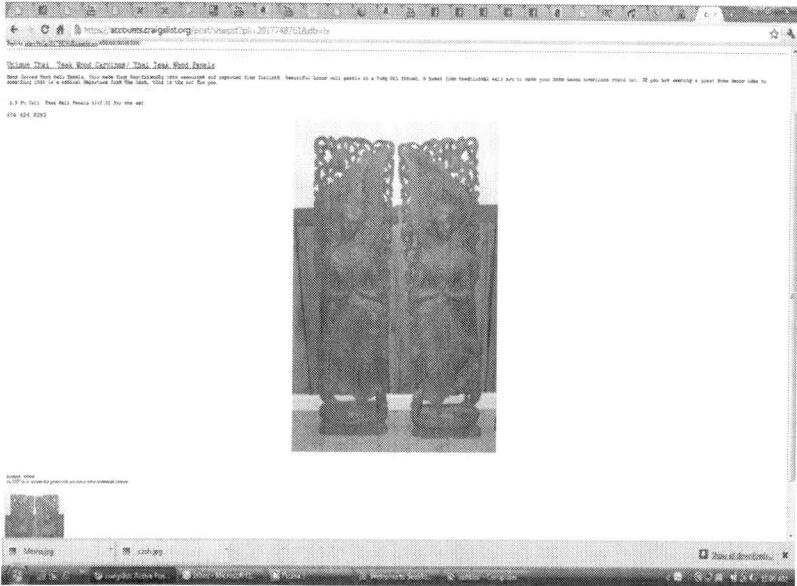

This screenshot is reduced by 50% to get as much of the image as possible in the window! Full size!

Now you see why I recommended this process. It is time consuming but worth the effort. This will make your Craigslist ads stand out and be significantly more effective!

ReCap!

*Clear pictures

*Several pictures

*Make sure your lighting makes the item look hot!

*Put text on the pictures, (say your customer service number and phone number)

*On jewelry, make sure the pictures are clear (outside lighting is great)

*Determine if the item is worth taking one picture of or not. Clothing—low-end, one shot, let it roll. Clothing—high-end, several different shots to increase your loot! There is a method for this also: on low-margin items, take one very good picture and let it roll. There is no reason to spend a lot of time on pictures of items that you will only collect a few dollars on. I like to do my tasks in groups; it creates flow and a sense of completion versus having a list of unfinished action items.

Clear, Clean, Concise

Now it is time for the fun part; time to prep your piles for the listing of your items online. If you currently buy or sell on eBay, you have seen very short and very long item descriptions. Go short, go very short; only put in what you need to put in, most folks barely read the shortest of descriptions. The rest is overkill, a waste of time and could cost you money. Have you ever heard that expression "putting lipstick on the pig"? Well, it is still a pig. I have seen many people try to "sell" a crappy item with a grand description.

eBay success is product driven and deal driven. Do not waste a lot time with long auction descriptions unless you are in a very specialized market, say antiques or some other rare item, then it is worth it. I once had an antique butcher's block, at that time I did not know much about butcher's blocks. In my quest to get rid of the butcher's block, I took several pictures and wrote a short description, put it up on eBay, it went for $500.00 and the feedback was not that high either. This section is going to be very short. Just remember: clear and accurate titles, clear and concise short item descriptions, and put in as many key words as you can, pertaining to the item that is being listed. No fancy templates—sometimes they are distracting and will cost you money.

There is one exception to this, if you have an e-commerce site, you are going to proceed a little differently. If you have your own site with your own template, I would use it (sans the domain stuff) so when they go there it is congruent. One thing that is different is you will put a phone number and your customer service email address in the body of the listing, the one with your domain name; yes, this is permissible. I often used eBay for lead generation. Have you ever seen a seller with a very nicely done eBay ad, but it does not look like much is going on? Well more than likely, if they have not given up on eBay, they are using the site to refer leads to their own site.

Trust me, it works. There are people who will go to eBay and because of the sometimes unfavorable impression many folks have about eBay; they will leave eBay and buy on your site! There is no magic bullet on this and it is not rocket science. I do not believe in trying to trick people to buy crappy items with flowery language. It is stupid and it doesn't work! The real trick to eBay is product sourcing—you've got to *get* a deal in order to sell it at a deal price or you will not make money. A word about feedback—everyone is overly concerned with feedback in my opinion. I have seen so many people lose it over feedback, saying things like, ***"I got to get my feedback to such and such place, to sell well."*** Nothing could be further from the truth! Focus on product research, great prices and excellent service and the feedback doesn't even matter! Feedback can be manipulated or gamed. Many people do not leave feedback on great deals. Bidders can and will use feedback as a bargaining chip. I do not know how many times I got an email that went like this, ***"thanks for the fast shipping but (insert any reason here) and I would like to know how to proceed before I leave feedback."*** If I knew we did nothing wrong and were accurate with the description, I would tell them to send it back. Yes! Send it back for a full refund. Most folks who are gamers are lazy, very lazy and 85% of those people kept the items and went away—many even left positive feedback.

The items that were sent back usually went for more the second time, not always but at least 75% of the time. With numbers like that I took chances and things went well. Make your own decision, because the ultra savvy bidder knows how to get their money back and keep the item if you do not act fast enough!

You have a Refund Policy you just did not know it!

I am going to give you some insight to how this happens. Believe it or not it is not PayPal! Nope! Shocking, I know! It is Visa, MasterCard, AMEX and Discover—in their contracts, it is stipulated that you must have a refund policy to use their services as a merchant.

So if you take those credit cards through PayPal, you in fact have **a de-facto refund policy regardless of what is on your terms of service section.** I know no one tells you these things—that is why I am here. But that is not the worst, the worst is the dreaded *"item is not as described"* that many consumers are putting in their disputes. This is the kiss of death; you cannot win unless you take them to court and you'd better have bulletproof evidence of your claim, otherwise, it is a waste of time and money.

With PayPal, when you get someone who puts *"item is not as described"* in as a dispute, as soon as you can, escalate the claim and offer a full refund once the item is returned. This will force them to return it. If you wait and they win, they get their money back and do not have to send the item back! At the start of my eBay career if someone was unhappy, you worked it out and they did not even involve PayPal. Now, they will put in a claim and then contact you. Too many claims place you on a list with PayPal and we are not talking double digits either.

The consumer is very savvy and some are unethical, yep I said it *"some consumers are unethical and will try to get over on you".* For the most part, 90% of the folks you deal with will be fine and if there is an issue, it really is an issue. But that other 10% —all I can do is shake my head. Once, we had a saddle up on eBay, sold it to this lady and she made all types of claims about the saddle. Said her son had to get a shot because of what was on the saddle. She put in a claim after I told her to send it back and we would give her a full refund. She felt she should have not had to go through the trouble of sending it back since we put her out.

About thirty minutes after I got off the phone with her, she put in the *"item is not as described"* claim, which I immediately escalated and said return it to get your money back—which she did. When I got it back, I found that it was never even opened! There is no 100% way to insulate yourself from nuts; you are going to have to deal with some of them. That is life! This is just some more information for you to better arm yourself with and protect your business. With online commerce growing, this problem will become larger. Now your hopes, dreams and profits are in the crosshairs of this wave. Better warned and prepared versus blindsided.

Looking Out For Number One! Going Gangsta!

Now that I have thoroughly frightened you, it is time to build you up. What is the most important thing in all of this? Well my friend it is you. It is not eBay and it is not the customers, because if you do not take care of you, those two will leave you very quickly. While you are building eBay's business you should be building your own.

Life is what you make it!

Here is the **Gangsta** move that will put a smile on your face. Create your own website or blog (you can sell on a blog, I do everyday) and lead those customers to your website. It doesn't matter if it is new or used, people will buy your items if the price is right and if it is what they want. Here is an excellent link for you if you never built a website www. 2createawebsite.com. I highly recommend the site—a good friend of mine, Lisa Irby, created it for people who never ever built one. This is definitely a great resource for you to build your site. Now it gets even better, while you are doing the website you can search out other opportunities to make money with eBay's customers!

Depending on what you sell and how much traffic you build, once it is built, you can sell ad space on your site. Link up to affiliate marketing and sell your other products to those folks you direct to your site from eBay! Look, eBay is the biggest pimp in the world; they make tons of money off your listing fees, PayPal and end of auction fees. Then, eBay will make changes to decrease your cash flow all in the name of protecting their bottom line.

If you think this method of marketing is unethical, so be it, I did it and made a lot of money off the traffic I got from eBay. I never lost a night of sleep. How do you do this? Remember in the beginning I said put your customer service phone number and email address with your website domain? That is the beginning. You also need to put your picture up—folks connect with people they can relate to. The next step is the www.craigslist.com hustle. You got your website up and running. Now it is time to direct more traffic from www.craigslist.com to your website and eBay listings. You can do direct links and or put the exact same verbiage from the eBay listing with a picture. You may or may not get flagged, but no worries, you are going to be doing this frequently. Once the eBay listing is done, just copy and paste the ad or the link.

This is where the magic happens. By using the same ad copy, phone number, email address and image on eBay, www.yourwebsite.com and www.craigslist.com, you will start to have your ads show up in Google much quicker. I found this out completely by accident. I was Googling my phone number and an ad I put up earlier in the day was already in Google! I went to my dashboard to find out what happened. I did not find anything on the website dashboard, next I went to Photobucket and there it was! With www.photobucket.com you can get the metrics on how often an image was hit. When you get 300 (maybe less) or more hits, it will populate you in Google rather quickly. I noticed after that spike, my sales numbers edged up by 12%. The easier you are to find in Google, the more money you can make.

What is awesome about this is, it is purely organic and will not bring in the Google police! Trying to game Google can get you blacklisted, which I find ironic, because paid search is actually gaming the system. Now we are cooking! After a few months, if you keep it up, even after your ads are deleted they will still be in Google with your phone number, website and email address for a while. All of this is marketing that will help you make more sales although sometimes, this does not happen.

Life is what you make it!

People on Craigslist will start calling you and asking if you have things they did not see, because you are now someone they have seen for more than a day. There is something about consistency that draws people to you. I kept getting calls for about three months after we closed the store! Good marketing takes time and consistency but it is well worth it! Have you ever noticed how eBay tries to alienate you from the bidder? Well, they look at those bidders as their customers buddy and you are just renting a virtual booth. By putting the methods I've mentioned in place, more of those customers will be able to contact you. Now what do you do with them?

Sell baby sell! I have noticed that some people who shop on eBay tend to be skittish and slightly paranoid when going outside of eBay. There are others who are veterans and can teach you the ropes. When they call you or email, close the deal! If they were not interested, they would not contact you. Quickly get to business and close the deal. The longer they have to think about it, the worse it is for your wallet. We, as Americans, can be quite fickle; this comes from living in the land of plenty and having endless options. This is not everyone but it does happen a lot in the world of sales.

Here are some hints to help steer the herd your way. In your listings I have found these lines to be very helpful in starting a sales conversation:

"If you have any questions about this item, call or email me"

"We will go the extra mile for you—to learn more about us, call or email us "

Life is what you make it!

"Please direct queries to 111-222-3333 or email us at getmoney@yourwebsite.com

"To learn more about our shipping process, call or email us"

"For a faster response, call our customer service number 111-222-3333"

You can use any variation of the statements above that you want, but always give the two options of a phone number and an email. I did this for years and got more grief from PayPal /eBay because I was selling well and making money. You can get away with this tactic as long as you're promoting excellent customer service; which you are—for yourself and your business—not eBay's! Now you can use your cell phone number if you like, but I prefer to use a Google Voice number which you can forward to any number you desire. Understand that by using these methods carefully and diligently, you can skirt the censure of eBay.

You can do anything you want; it is how you do it that matters.

Another operation for quicker sales on eBay is the double duty—every item you have listed on eBay, you also have listed on Craigslist—this is how you do it. As I stated earlier, get yourself a Gmail account for the ton of nifty features such as the Picasa photo album where you can take pictures and put the same information in the album, get the link from the album, insert the link in a Craigslist listing and you have yet another source of sales. When you use this technique, you will receive responses from two groups of people. One will say ***"I saw it on eBay"*** This group you can ignore. The second group will approach with offers to buy or offer you a better deal. These are the people that you want to work with.

Section Review:

*You are intentionally steering traffic from eBay to your website or Craigslist ads and vice versa.

*You are creating points of conversation to convert eBay customers to your customers.

*You will create a website / blog to push your items for profit.

*You are posting the same items on your website, eBay and Craigslist all at the same time.

Free Stuff

Many times, landlords have to evict people or the people leave and often they leave sellable stuff. You will be amazed by what people leave. Yes, there will be some trash, but hey it's free stuff. Offer to pick it up. You can go cheap and say you will do it for $25.00—they are either going to do it or hire someone anyway. What would you do to find these freebies? I will keep it simple; you can go to any classified section that has things for sale and make deals. Most folks are lazy so if you're asking enough people and offering something in return, you will get decent to great inventory for nearly free. That is pimping the classifieds. Ask and ye shall receive!

Cash In When You Can—local pickups

This section is for larger items. You will come across many very large items in your search for products. Many of these items can be sold for a great profit! Here is the trick, you got to have a space to store it and of course you need to move it. You can sell big items on eBay just as easy as the smaller items. Once the desirability factor kicks in, if it is hot and priced right it will sell, even on eBay. This is a chance to get "cash" off an eBay sale— saving you PayPal fees. On the pickups you have to make arrangements with the buyer and when they asked me if I wanted the cash when they came to pickup or PayPal, I always took the cash!

As you get more experience, you will be able to spot deals quickly. Many of you already have certain levels of knowledge about items such as tools, medical equipment, cars, which will be helpful—*I once sold a 1957 Chevy Truck Body on eBay, it was rusty and I got $750 for it; my cost, had I had to haul it off.*

If you have a smart phone you may be able to get the information you need right on the spot!

Do not be afraid of the larger items; appliances can be bought cheaply off eBay and resold at a profit on Craigslist. I have done it but you need cheap access to a truck. Same rules apply as well for the smaller stuff, and if you prefer, you can have them bring you cash upon pickup. Cash doesn't bounce nor does it get charged-back! Just something to think about—everyone shies away from larger stuff looking for small, cheap and convenient. I bought a unit that had a very old printing press in it, very large and heavy. Got offered a $1.00—the printer, it later turns out, was worthless for resale online; however, the printer and all of the metal in the unit brought $650 at the scrap yard. We had to take it apart to move it! You never know in this business, something that was junk online was worth quite a bit locally.

Furniture is my favorite product to sell (deep furniture, back ground, commercial and residential). Thousands of people sell millions of dollars worth of furniture on Craigslist for cash every year and it moves well. With that said, do not be afraid of furniture. Crappy, smelly and otherwise undesirable furniture yes, be afraid and run fast from that stuff! But something nice, you can work it out, it is all a matter of price. Here, in Atlanta, people have just given me nice stuff or my guys saw nice stuff on the curb and brought it back to the store. I cannot over emphasize how I am amazed at what people throw away!

PayPal Management

I would be remiss to not bring this up; PayPal is going to be a big part of this process. If you are a seasoned seller, you should be good to go, but never, ever keep a lot of money in your PayPal account. Reason being, if they limit it, they have nothing! Number two, have a sweep checking account. The PayPal deposits go into your bank account and you move (sweep) them to another account that PayPal does not have access to. This will keep you from waking up to a very unpleasant surprise of finding your money gone! If you do everything you need to do in terms of keeping customers happy you should not have a problem, but why take chances? Yes, I am very paranoid when it comes to PayPal.

If you do not want to give up your social security number, (initially you will not have to), but if you start processing many sales, expect the "review" to come up. I went through it every time I changed categories and my sales went through the roof. You can start a LLC (cheap) get an EIN and give them that number. You will need to be in Dun & Bradstreet, to make that fly, for at least three months, for them to pull a credit check on your business. If you do not have an EIN, you are going to have to give up the SSN to get the account unlocked. How to avoid the dreaded review: you need to be a good boy or girl for six months, no disputes or issues.

You will also need to keep your sales steady and consistent (hence my preference for getting cash when you can). If you have a spike, say you are doing $1500–$3000 a month and you go to $10,000 a week, they will be calling you! If you do not answer the phone they will limit you. As you may recall from an earlier Chapter, this has happened to me four times and it is always when I was growing my business. Each time I got through it, but it is a "pucker" moment (a moment of desperation) when you've got $12,000.00 that you need and cannot get access to. Got through it and did not lose a customer, but in my opinion this review needs to be done before-hand not when you are in the midst of growing your business. So be very careful with PayPal and the people who never had a problem with PayPal I guarantee you they were not running $50-65K a month through PayPal. I know I have beat this dead horse before, but you have an opportunity to make this type of money off one unit—that is the power of storage auction units.

Life is what you make it!

The more you sell the more issues you will encounter. That was a very large exposure level for PayPal and I was a small business so the scrutiny was definitely there. Handle customer disputes as quickly as possible; most people are reasonable—very reasonable and the nuts are, well, nuts! If the item in dispute is something you got for free and you can to live with the loss, refund the money and move on. If it is an item of significant value make them return it. When a bidder does a dispute and you do not think you can work with them, escalate the claim and say you will refund all of their money after they return it. This way you will not lose out!

As soon as you can, get the PayPal debit card; you can withdraw up to $400.00 cash per day—it is much faster than a transfer. I am amazed at how many people, who are long time ebayers, do not have the debit card. You can get up to two. There you have it, some of my techniques that will enable you to get products and navigate the world of eBay and win!

The System

This section is for someone that wants to build a network of ebay-ers to do all of the heavy lifting. This is what I did in my last phase of eBay. I really enjoyed scouting out deals and going to storage unit auctions, so I had to make a choice —either go to fewer auctions and help out with the listings or hire someone. We tried hiring someone and that did not go over too well. I knew the money was in the buying— there are deals out there! So attending fewer auctions was not going to work!

One day, I went on eBay and found some local sellers who didn't appear to be busy; I emailed them with this pitch:

"I can give you more stuff than you can handle. I will bring it to you, you list, you ship and once you get paid just hold on to the cash for me to pick up. You will make 20% on the sales."

They all said 30–35%. I said no, too much for what I would bring them. One relented and said she needed the money and it was getting harder for her to do the listing and find items. I set up a meeting (I also took a box truck worth of stuff). Anne was pleasant and quite industrious. I liked her immediately! We hit it off and I had her sign the contract and we began that day. She started listing and selling that day and within a week she had made what she normally made in a month! She still had items to list!

You could say Anne was more than happy; she was making more money and she did not have to source product. I had Anne send me a screen shot of her PayPal account before she met me and after she started listing our stuff. I sent the screen shots to all of the people who said no and asked them if they would take 15% to get a piece of the action, which they all did (a week later I bumped them up to the 20%) So we had five new eBay horses pulling the cart and my partner listed the really high end stuff, so we became a logistics company. There was more effort in shipping and transport than anything else!

This move enabled us to reach the $60–$70K per month in sales mark for the first time. It would not have happened otherwise. You have a lot of folks that do eBay and do it well. Their biggest problem is sourcing sellable products. As I've said so many times over, it is the products, not some cute little gimmick that will help you make money on eBay. As you can tell from the book, there are so many ways to make money with eBay; it can boggle the mind. Understand that this is a journey, and enjoy yourself along the way. eBay is still a great place to make money, no doubt about it. You can, with strategy, hard work and effort, make a great deal of money on eBay, even now! It just helps to know what you are getting into. I wrote this book to help you get the most profit possible, which means getting a screaming deal on your entire inventory, which you can do. People forget there were great property deals before the recession and there always will be deals in the United States of America—believe in that.

The Craigslist Hustle

As I call it, is a great way to resale your storage auction finds. Craigslist is a wonderful resource to move products and even make friends! Craigslist is a dynamic set of communities that is always on and open. As you can tell I love Craigslist! In our best year, we sold **$385,000** dollars worth of merchandise on Craigslist alone. When I say you can make money on Craigslist, I am not kidding! Even now, with the economy as it is. I recently sold some things out of my home; everything was gone in four hours! This is how you do it. Since Craigslist moves so fast, re-listing your items is a necessary evil if it does not sell the first time. There are a few pitfalls to frequent relisting:

YOU WILL GET FLAGGED

Please know it is coming and do not sweat it, nor take it personally—it is part of the game. Just keep posting your items and making money. If you are a low volume seller, you may not run into this problem. You will need three to four different email accounts and two to three different ISP's if you get banned like I did for over posting (about 30-40 or more items a day, five days a week). Even with that, I was still posting and getting people in the store! Why the flagging?

There are people who are addicted to Craigslist and they log in every day expecting to see new stuff. When they keep seeing your postings they get pissed and flag you. Yes, it is that simple. I have even had a job posting flagged because the individuals felt that it did not pay enough; as some idiots wrote to explain the finer points of job offers and compensation to me. Go figure!

To get the full benefits of Craigslist, you will need a camera, HTML editor **(SeaMonkey is free—see TOOLS of the Trade section)**, a Picasa account (it comes with a Gmail email account), a Photobucket account and a phone number. Remember, I use my Google voice numbers only for online businesses which means when it rings, it is about money! You need to learn how to price your items; it is part science and art. If your item is priced too high, it will sit, if it is priced too low, you feel ripped off when it sells so fast. So do a quick market analysis of what is up on Craigslist. If you have an item that is rare or not found easily (chaise lounge, corner cabinet, etc.) you can price higher; if it is a common item, bomb the price and get rid of it! If most of the beds up on Craigslist are, say, $150–$200 dollars in price, then you should price your bed at $125.00 if it came out of a unit, and unless you got caught up, you paid next to nothing for it. Remember, speed and efficiency are the keys to making money in this business.

Answer the phone when would be buyers call; people lose their minds on Craigslist. If they want your item, lock down the deal ASAP. Please believe that when they are on the phone with you they are still looking on Craigslist for the item you have for sale—it is like an addiction. In their minds, someone may have just put a better deal up. Sometimes it does happen just like that! Your pictures are more important than the description; you want the best shots possible. I always included other items I was selling in the background in my shots, sold a lot of stuff that way. Keep your descriptions short, most folks do not read long descriptions so it is pointless and a waste of time.

Once you have taken pictures of all your items for sale, load the pictures in Photobucket and Picasa—many people thought my Picasa photo album was a website—that is how good it is. Now that your pictures are loaded, you can do one ad with pictures from Photobucket.com. This will give you unlimited pictures for your ad, compared to the four you get with Craigslist's picture loader. Not to mention, you can track hits on your items. If you get three to four hundred hits and you are not getting any phone calls, then your price is too high. Make the adjustment and sell your item. It is information like that which gives you power versus selling in a vacuum. The beauty of using a Picasa is, it is easy to maintain. I find it super easy to add more or to delete the items as they sell. This is an old one I just found, it give you an idea of what I was doing every week.

http://picasaweb.google.com/upscale66/SOLDITEMS#

The Picasa tool makes it easy to relist a lot of items. Just insert the link in the ad, post and click and you are done. You are going to launch not one but a series of ads in the same categories' at different times of the day. Why?

Your ad will get buried in a matter of minutes in the larger cities and we live in an immediate gratification world. Word to the wise: post your item or items every hour on the hour —at least three times a day, at a minimum and be sure to remove your ads once your item sells. It is like picking up garage sale signs after the sale—a form of simple courtesy.

Many erroneously assume that the items sell the first day. Often the things will sell that fast but if they are priced wrong, they can be on the site until they expire. **Here is a money tip!** Go back a few weeks on the section of Craigslist you are shopping /selling in and call up or email people about the item they had for sale. More than **50%** will still have the items! I have bought items from people on Craigslist, turned around and sold it for more in a matter of hours. Remember, 90% of the people selling on Craigslist are casual, one-shot, sellers. They are not going to put in the time and effort that you will in the business. Offer delivery options; there are a lot of single women who shop Craigslist who do not have help and this will make the deal for them. Service is a great thing in new or resell world. I eventually got out of the delivery side and outsourced my deliveries. There are several people who advertise delivery services in the furniture section; it will not be hard to find someone. If you really want the item gone, just put delivery included within a certain square mileage—this will help tremendously to move your product.

Shipping can kill you!

This will be a short but critical section. You have great stuff, and you are selling it on eBay, major online book seller sites, and your website, like hotcakes and then, boom! You get the email.

"When are you shipping my item? I have not gotten it yet and it has been over two weeks."

Sometimes this email is polite and sometimes you can see their head spinning around as they write the email. I can understand why they are upset, no doubt about that. When the post office loses your customer's package, it can be a long day! Well, they really do not lose the shipment, (rare but it does happen) for the most part. What can happen is that it can be delayed and your buyer is emailing and calling you!

We have had packages take anywhere from three weeks to four months to arrive. This puts you in a serious bind with your customer and PayPal, whose policy states: all items must be shipped in a timely manner. The customers can get a full refund and keep your item when it finally shows up! This is what can happen to you if you do not adhere to these guidelines that are set forth in PayPal's terms of service. So I advise you to use UPS or FedEx as much as possible; yes, they lose and damage things also, but they are a hell of a lot easier to work with, in terms of getting money for damages, than the USPS!

It is an ugly position to be in for you and your business. eBay and PayPal are looking at your customer service ratings like never before; this can tank your ratings, therefore, costing you time and money. If you have an eBay Powerseller rating, you can lose it over shipping issues alone. You are screwed with the United States Postal Service! We have used every shipping service there is, if you have volume and I hope you will have huge volume in your business, there are going to be shipping issues from time to time. Things will be damaged, customers will lie (not many but a few) that they did not get the item, or items are delivered to the wrong address. There is nothing that you have done or can do to prevent this from happening! That is why I am breaking it down on how to protect your interests in the event that something like this does happen to you. If you use the USPS, always send your item with delivery confirmation and make sure that your item is taped up well.

Be proactive. Every day or every other day, check to see if the item was delivered—this is also a good time to ask for the feedback. One note, at times the USPS can be painfully slow updating their tracking website. Your buyer will leave you feedback and it is still pending in the USPS website. One thing about the USPS is they provide free boxes for flat rate priority shipping, which can be a grand thing. Save you money on shipping supplies and aren't those your tax dollars at work? We have not had that many issues with the priority service, however unless there is enough profit on the item, most items are not going priority. Understand, until the item reaches the buyer, the package is your responsibility, come hell or high water. Here is a good tip, say you have a buyer who is unhappy and wants a refund plus the returned cost of shipping it back to you and he or she is being nasty. You know you are getting negative feedback. Many times, these people want their money and do not want to worry about trudging through the snow to mail the item back to you. As I have stated before, when they file their PayPal claim, you go in and escalate the claim by saying you will refund their money once the item is returned which forces them to send the item back to get a refund. More than half go away at this point. Know that you are going to have some problem customers. Yes, I said problem customers. Make a decision based on the impact on your business. If you made a mistake, own up to it, most folks can deal with and respect you for the honesty.

Shipping Tips

Make your shipping as cheap as possible! I cannot say this enough! Ship it as fast as you can—speedy shipping leads to speedy feedback. Use the best boxes you can for shipping, it is your image. Double box fragile items and cover the item with a layer of peanuts—this method saved a merino glass parrot from ruin.

Go international; it is not that hard. We have had more problems with domestic shipping. I would suggest Global priority; 8–10 days it is worth it! Surprise your buyers; if you make a lot of money on a storage unit auction item—splurge for the upgraded shipping—in the long run it is well worth it. Do not be afraid to work the local pickup options on smaller items. If you have a store, it will increase sales.

Putting flat rate shipping in your ads saves you time and emails.

Always insure anything over one hundred dollars whether the customers pays for it or not. If things get funky, you are covered. Never, ever ship anything without delivery confirmation!

Always buy your shipping supplies in bulk; we have ULINE shipping supplies and packing materials in Atlanta—love these guys!

Once you have established volume, you can get a discount with either UPS or FEDEX which will be a two for one deal. You save money and earn money at the same time. When we converted, we started earning one to five dollars off of shipping. This was a nice little chunk of change! Average earning was $225 times $1,000 plus in sales a month. It is something to keep in mind while you are working your business. Plan for growth and you will have growth.

Inventory Management

Okay, you are buying and selling storage units and by now you have noticed how quickly you have run out of room. It can happen to you before you know it! If you bought two big units, you might be covered up and not even be aware of how much stuff you have until it is around your neck!

Here are some tips and guidelines to ease this problem. Number one, you have got to get low margin and worthless items out of your mix as quick as possible. You soon will become an expert at inventory triage. First thing, nail down all of your big items, furniture, refrigerators, washers and dryers, sofa sets, dining room set and bedroom sets—get them on eBay and Craigslist ASAP! They are big and they take up the most room and they usually make nice coin, depending on how old and hot they are in the marketplace.

Do these tasks before you start to address the small stuff— you can spend a whole day sorting and missing out on the sale of the larger items. I am a big believer in multi-tasking! Once you have your larger items in the sales channel, (unless they need repairs- I will cover that later) start going through your inventory—you will have three piles or stacks. In one stack, you will have your eBay items based on pricing thresholds you established earlier on. The other stack will be your major online book seller items such as books, CD's and other items you have determined you can sell on these sites. Remember, in the beginning I said to start familiarizing yourself on these selling platforms, now you know why. It is very time consuming to list, sort and search!

The last stack is your dump stack or free stack. In this stack will be trash, of course, and items you know are not worth selling or you can't sell because of space restrictions. Here are your options: trash it, donate it or give it away. I found that a very good way to move items is to mix in some low margins items with the junk and post the entire lot on Craigslist. Yes, I love Craigslist! I have made a lot of money off Craigslist! You can too. As you put items up on eBay, **major online book seller** sites and Craigslist, it will help to have a dedicated area for your online businesses for answering questions and shipping.

Once you become entrenched in the business, you will be surprised at how much stuff for your business you will get —I am talking office furniture, storage totes, book shelves, shipping supplies, scales, pallets the whole nine yards. Depending on how much space you have, you can give stuff to your customers as a gift for shopping with you. People love free stuff; the more the better! I used to run an ad on Craigslist free section every week, it was awesome to move that stuff out of the mix!

Do not let stuff stack up and think you will get to it later!

I was guilty of this early on in the business; it did not cost me money but it did delay money. Our focus was furniture, accent pieces, electronics and appliances; we had a section of the warehouse that we would let items stack up mostly boxes and clothing. We were pulling stuff out of the stacks, but it was growing faster than we could nibble on it. One day I could not take it anymore, I made it a goal to tame the beast and reclaim that warehouse space. I started going through the stacks and was amazed at how much stuff was in those boxes. I started coming across valuable eBay items, almost immediately. I found a sterling flatware set, some Roseville pottery, Le Crueset pots, some costume jewelry, a lot of broken gold, a set of BMW X5 Rims and tires, some antiques and more. We had ten thousand square feet in the warehouse and this area must have been almost two thousand square feet! I know what I speak of when I say it can accumulate very quickly.

The key component to this business is flow, and the management of flow—cash flow and inventory flow. Too much, and you are overwhelmed, and not enough, you are scrambling for inventory. You want to be a little overwhelmed, just enough so that the pressure will push you to sell more and sell it faster.

There is nothing like the incentive of making more money to crack the whip on your hind parts. I am not going into specific office setups, everyone is going to have a different situation and I am not bright enough to think of every conceivable possibility in this business for someone else. There are just too many variables. I will say this: you want your work area to be clean and orderly. You are going to need some space to keep your paperwork straight.

Hold-itis is worse than bad breath

Hold-itis—*a condition where you are deluding yourself to the true value of the merchandise on hand.* "

Once you get in this business, price and value are going to be constant themes in your life. Do not get too caught up in blue book value, your uncle Roy or what a website says this item is worth, be it x or y. What it is worth is what someone is willing to pay you for it, **NOW!**

The reason that I'm addressing this syndrome is because it is rampant!   We, as Americans, have a strange preoccupation with expected value, and what we think we should get as payment for whatever item, service or deed that we perform.   Value is like water—dynamic and fluid, subject to change based on a number of variables.

One glaring example of this statement is what is happening to the residential and commercial real estate markets.   If you had told anyone, living in the United States in the year of 2005 that their home which was valued at $350,000 in 2005 would be worth $180,000 today in 2010, that person and anyone that was in the range of your voice, would have thought that you were as dumb as hell.

The truth of the matter, real estate prices dip and rise with the events of the world. The prices of real estate have been depressed before, in the future it will appreciate, and in the future it will be depressed again.   Everything is cyclical; sometimes the price that you get for an item is beyond anything that you can do. When you are in the process of developing your business plan, a common theme that will emerge is the requirement for consistent cash flow. This is the most important thing in your business; as long as you have constant cash flow that covers your expenses, you're in a position to grow your business.   Cash flow to your business is like food is to your body—without it, your business will die. Now that I have sufficiently frightened you, the gist of this conversation, is to prepare you to learn how to acknowledge and accept certain marketplace dynamics.   What the item was worth last year is the irrelevant to what it is worth today.

Life is what you make it!

Your main objective is to maintain a consistent cash flow and make a profit on the items you are obtaining from the storage units. Hold-itis will impede that effort like a disease impedes the quality of life; please do not become infected with hold-itis. It is harmful to your financial health!

There are very few items worth holding on to for the extended period of time. I will give you a few scenarios to work with. Rare, high grade antiques, are worth holding on to. You will not be able to sell these items in your regular selling channel and realize full financial value. Authentic and critically acclaimed artwork is in the same boat; these type of items need to be put in a proper place in order to realize their true value. Period pieces, many things can be period pieces: a chair, an iron, a clock—far too many things to go into in this space. When you're conducting your due diligence and researching items, that is when you discover what these things may be; at that juncture, you will make the assessment whether this is an item that you should hold onto. Now ask yourself this question,

"Why am I holding on to this item?"

"Is it for my kids?"

"Will I take it to a proper auction later on in the year?"

"Am I waiting on Christmas when this item will do very well?"

"Is there a really good chance that this item will appreciate if I hold on to it for two to three years?"

As you read these questions, something should become very evident. There should be a purpose for holding on to an item. That purpose should be well defined and if at all possible, should have a timetable. 95% of the items that you will pull out of a storage auction unit will not meet the rare, high-end value criteria. Is it possible that you may pull a **Jackson Pollock** out of a unit? Yes, it is possible. Rich people, that are frivolous with their money, often go bust and lose their stuff, more so than the average American that has less than 1/100 of the countries wealth! It happens every day! This syndrome is the reason that I named my blog:

-Urbanpackrat –

Many storage auction buyers become pack rats; holding on to items without any rhyme or reason. What happens to these people is they start to hoard stuff, mirroring their thoughts and dreams to their possessions. Almost living a fantasy life by virtue of what they own vs. the people that they are. One of the older veterans of the storage auction game told me this story. He owned a house up in Lawrenceville, Georgia. In this house he stored all of the gold that he collected out of storage units for, *at that time,* the last 10 years!

My eyes popped out of my head! If he was getting gold as frequently as I was, we were talking six figures in the value of the gold that he had in the house. Well, the house was not in the best condition, which is shocking since he was storing something very valuable in the house. I shared the thought that crossed my mind with him; he said that was part of his security plan. No one would think anything of that type of value would be in the house like that. I nodded my head, it did make sense.   While he was out of the country on an international trip, the house suffered damage in a storm. When he got back, he found out that the house had been bulldozed!

He was out of his mind when he went to look at the property. It was his, he still owned it. The house was gone, and in its place was just a patch of dirt. He was depressed for a long time over that. On that day, I vowed that would never happen to me.   Going forward, I made judicious selling plans and the longest time that I held on to an item that I personally wanted to keep, was six months.

As for my friend, I personally think someone stole his gold and created the situation to hide the crime. Most counties are very slow to move on dilapidated houses. Sometimes they stand for years if not decades, before someone addresses the situation.   The moral of this story is to safeguard your valuables and have an active, realistic plan to sell them—if you're not holding on to them for family keepsakes.

Remember, speed and efficiency will make you money; this is a marathon not a sprint.

11

Solutions for Apartment Dwellers

You have been watching my videos on YouTube and reading my blog, **"What Not to Leave in a Storage Unit"** and have decided that becoming a professional storage auction buyer is something that you want to do. You are full of enthusiasm and you even have a little change jingling in your pocket; however, there's one little roadblock. You live in an apartment, townhouse are some other place that does not have a lot of space. Since you are a smart cookie, you know that you will require space to be successful in this business.

This section is just for you!

Note: this program was designed for someone that was unemployed, so he had the time to devote to this business. Please make adjustments based on your situation.

One of my webinar attendees lived in an apartment. He found it very challenging to do the things that are required to be successful in the storage auction business. Not to mention his neighbors were exceptionally nosey. It was clearly spelled out in his lease; he could not run a business from his apartment. We put our heads together and developed this plan. You could buy one unit; the best unit you can get your hands on but this may max out your budget. No worries, we have a different game plan for you.

There is a certain method to the madness—because you are in a situation where you lack space, there will be some duplicate work involved. The first course of action is to buy a unit, depending on where you are in the process of prepping yourself for the business. Once you buy that first unit, the size and what is in that unit determines your next step.

For this exercise, we will make the assumption that you bought a 10 x 20 and it is full, from the roota to the toota. This unit is packed so tight, you cannot even slide a thought in there. You will take full advantage of the 24 to 72 hours that most storage facilities give you to clean out the unit. On the second day, call up the storage facility and inform them of your intent to rent the unit, this way they will not reserve the unit for someone else in their automated system.

After securing the unit, the next day or perhaps that day depending on how much time you have on your hands, you will begin to remove what looks like trash, things that you cannot sell, the items that you promised to return to the delinquent tenant, (things such as bibles, birth certificates, Social Security cards and so on and so forth). Once you gather all of that stuff, take it to the storage facility's office for the renter to retrieve. It may be a few days before you can take everything to the rental office. Many folks have their personal papers scattered throughout the unit.

You will need room to operate; each day you will do a little bit of clearing space. In some cases, you may have to rent another unit to place the smaller stuff in, while you sell the larger items. Once you have enough room to see what you have in your unit, you will begin placing these items in your sales channels. **Your goal is to sell the largest items first.** The clock is ticking; you want to have this unit almost cleaned out before it is time to pay rent again. In many regards, this process will be the exact reverse of many of the things I have spelled out in the book—because you do not have space, you have to crawl before you can walk—that is why there will be some incongruent themes in this section of the book.

You will save the eBay and Major Online Book Seller items for later. There's a plan for those items. Your immediate focus is to move the biggest items as fast as you can! For the larger items, you will begin to place them on Craigslist to liquidate them. There are some steps to this process. Before you sell anything, you want to make sure that you have everything that is part of that set. Many people stack their units when loading those units in a very strange manner. The chairs to a table set may be in the back and the table in the front, or vice versa. You will need to do an inventory before you sell anything. It all depends on how the unit is stacked.

Another prime example of this, would be the headboard and foot board of a bedroom set are in the front of the unit, while the rails and the rest of the bedroom set are in a very back of the unit. This happens a lot! You cannot sell the bedroom set until you have all of the pieces together, ensure that everything works and there's no damage. In many cases, you will have to pull everything out of the unit to conduct inventory and to take pictures.

The next step would be to take pictures. You will refer to **Chapter 5—Tools of Trade** to begin selling the large items. In many regards, this will be your part time job and you will be going to the unit to meet people and sell the items. To prepare yourself for this process, you will need the following items: **A camera, cell phone, a stack of legal pads and a laptop with a wireless connection—all of your work will be done away from your home.**

The reason why you should do this is unless you live very close to the storage facility where you bought your unit, there will be a lot of traveling back and forth. You're better off treating this as a fulltime job (that is if you do not have one) and setting up camp in a coffee shop or any business that has **Wi-Fi.** You put yourself in that position to respond rapidly to a buyer that wants to see something and you will be more productive working away from home. Most people are. This also changes your mindset about what you are doing; treat it like a business and it will act like a business.

This will create a separation between home and work. As someone that has been self employed for the last 10 years, it can become claustrophobic if you live and work in the same place all of the time. If your schedule does not permit this type of full-time commitment, work the process in the same manner, just on a part time basis. This would be your off day, or the weekends.

For stage two, we will assume that you have sold half of the big stuff and now have half of the unit to work out of. At this juncture, you will reassess the unit. It is time to look into the balance sheet. Thus far, after the money that you spent to buy the unit and paid rent, you now have a profit of $600. The breakdown is as follows:

Unit Cost = $650.00

- Rent $195.00

+ Sales $1445.00

= Profit $600.00

So far, so good you have a profit of $600; you have reset your capital, and you have rent for next month. This is very important; you just have created a business that is paying for itself.

The beauty of this plan is now you have a few items to sell on eBay and the major online book seller sites, which you're still not going to put on either site, not just yet—there's more work to do.

The next leg of the journey for you is to attend another auction and buy the best unit that you can with the money that you have, which is $1250. You will do this as soon as possible—a repeat of the process, step by step, that you did with the first unit. You now have your second unit; you immediately begin placing the larger items on Craigslist and making money as fast as you can. This unit cost you $1000 and the rent is $150 **(there is a wide disparity in storage unit rent pricing)**

You still have items that you're selling from the first unit. Now you are busier than ever, moving your larger items. The second unit has even more eBay and Major Online Book Seller site items. As you clean out the first unit, you will begin to move all of the eBay and Major Online Book Seller items from the second unit into the first unit.

You will not fill up the first unit; you will leave yourself 5 feet in the front and clear pathways from the front to the back of the unit. Once you get to this juncture, you will begin setting up your eBay and Major Online Book Seller businesses. Now things are percolating, you're still selling items from the first unit and slowly you're adding items to eBay and Major Online Book Seller.

You're keeping daily tallies of your cash flow and now is time to reassess both units. The first unit is full of online sales merchandise, which has a suggested sales value of $2500. Typically you move 20%–30% of the merchandise that you have on hand during a one week timeframe. That is $500-$750 dollars per week. You now have total sales of $1950 dollars from selling most of the big stuff out of the second unit and you still have things to sell! You are up $800.00 and next week your eBay and Major Online Book Seller accounts will pay you between $500-$750.00 and you have reset your buying budget! You have $1950.00 to buy!

The next step is to fully clean out unit two—that is why you left space in the first unit. You'll continue to move the large items as fast as you can. Since you have made a healthy profit; you can be very flexible in your pricing of the items that you have left and still make a profit! That is the beauty of storage auction units.

Stage three, you will continue to buy and sell in the manner that you have been over these last two units. Except there will be a new wrinkle. Now that you're selling items online through your **Major Online Book Seller** account and eBay account, shipping is now part of your life. This is how you will achieve that and not lose your mind. Most storage facilities do not have electrical power access to many of their units and if you do not have a mobile air card or **Clear** wireless Internet service, you will have to do the reconciling and printing of your labels and invoices somewhere else.

You will create a small shipping area in the unit, and stock it with shipping supplies. When you have an order, you will print up the invoice and take it with you to the unit. It may be a stack of invoices, the process is the same. You will wrap and hand label your packages. **Do not try to remember what is in each box**. *Confucius say, short pencil is better than long memory.* After all your packages are wrapped up and ready to go, just head to the United States postal service, FedEx or UPS and ship your customers their goods. This will be a little bit more extensive than if you were able to do it all in one place. So you now have a thriving online business.

Stage four. Invariably there will be good items in each unit that you cannot sell online. Every two weeks, or once a month, you will attend your local flea market as a vendor. Your intent is a little different than the other vendors. Your goal is to get rid of everything that you take to the flea market. This means you are going to be very flexible on price and whenever anyone makes you an offer, you will take it. Why? You were going to throw this stuff away anyway! It is found money! With the mindset that you are just getting rid of it, two things will happen, you will sell most of it and you will make money. Remember, your intent is not a gross sale, your intent is to get rid of everything and go back home with an empty truck.

Let's recap, you're buying and selling the contents of storage units. You have a thriving online business and you are regularly attending the flea market. You make money in all three channels. You're now a professional storage auction buyer! Your next goal is to get a house. You do not have to buy one, but you will be in a position now to rent one. This will add another selling channel to your arsenal to make more money. At this point, you have developed some very good habits. You're disciplined, organized and a good planner.

This is the method which moved my webinar attendee from a one bedroom apartment. He recently moved to a four bedroom, three baths, two-car garage home, with his rent only going up by $125! It took him seven months to pull this off; he is planning on opening a store next year. Now he is able to do everything that is outlined in the book. He currently has 8 storage units that he works out of! The only difference now is, the eBay and major online book seller items go to his home and he has one bedroom completely filled with over 6,000 books and over 1,200 CDs! He is making more money now than he ever has in his life!

12

Auction Houses

There is much talk about auction houses these days. I have used auction houses on several occasions to move specific merchandise. Years ago, I rented several booths in an antique store. My merchandise was occupying 38% of the store, maybe 40%. The owner of the antique store was retiring; she decided to sell everything in the store at an auction house. I was a little sick of the antique business; it is a different type of animal and you really need to love antiques to do well in it. I took this as an opportunity to get out and sell my stock very quickly.

My storage auction business was making money hand over fist and I really never spent any time over there **"refreshing"** my booths. We met with several auctioneers, found one that we liked, picked him and decided to sell our stuff through his auction house. Over a period of 60 days, he continued to run the merchandise that was left through future auctions; I made $22,000. The auction house is a good way to move a lot of merchandise very quickly.

Selling your items obtained from storage auctions at auction houses is not a cut and dry process. Like anything in life, there's a certain amount of politics that is involved with auction houses. The prime spots, which would be the first position, the second position, and the third position, (your position are spots), is when you will be allowed to sell your items in the auction house during auction night. Why is this important? Many auction houses have a regular crowd and most people show up for the first position and hang around until the third position. After that, two things occur, either they have run out of money, or they leave. Going later in the auction lineup can be detrimental to your financial success. There are exceptions—it could be a very big auction and an all day event—that is well advertised and plenty of buzz has been generated about this auction. You can do well at any spot that you are in. However, these auctions are run a little differently.

At the big auction, the all day event, your items will be run through whether you are there are not. At the smaller auction houses, you will be required to show up on auction day and unload your truck— bringing the items that you have for sale into the auction house. Some places may have help and other places you will be required to handle everything yourself. The only thing that the auction house is providing, which is a very important thing, is a venue for you to present your items up for sale.

Absolute Auction

There are three types of auctions: public outcry auction— this is the one that most people are familiar with; silent auction or sealed bid—this is an auction where you write down what you are willing to bid for the item; and thirdly, an auction with a reserve. An auction is reserved at a minimum purchase price; as you can understand, most people hate these auctions and they do not drum up a lot of response. The item must be super special for people not to be turned off by the reserve unless the reserve is very low and reasonable.

An absolute auction is the type of auction where there is no reserve and whatever final bid is received, is accepted. Many auction goers love these types of auctions! The reason is clear; they have a very good chance to score a super deal. If the item that is up for auction does not have at least two bidders that really want that item, it could literally go for $1.00! I have seen it! That is one of the reasons that I attended auctions; as a resale store owner, I was able to buy items at such a great discount that it was easy to mark the item up and make a profit in my store.

With that thought, know that when you sell your items at auction it is a very dicey proposition. You may have that one little odd item that many people go gaga over and make a lot of money. It happens. Overall, items sold at auction typically go for much less than you would make in a resale environment. **If that is the case why sell at auction?** One word—**speed.** You can sell literally a truck load of items in 30 minutes. I will give you an example; I have a very good friend that routinely sells his merchandise at these types of auctions. I have seen him buy a unit for $500, sell the best items out of the unit **(you cannot sell everything at an auction house)** and a few days later, make $1500, $2500, $3000 in less than an hour.

The Downside

There is a draw, your items are selling for less but you're selling more and you're selling faster. These are some of the drawbacks of selling in the auction house. It is very easy to become addicted to the fast money; long-term, if this is your only sales channel, you will be leaving a significant amount of money on the table. My objective to selling at the auction house was to move items that are very unique and are not doing very well in my store. I have always used auction houses in that manner; this is not to say that selling in the auction house would not be a great asset to you. For me, it was an add-on, a needed sales channel. I made more money, granted it took longer, but I could live with that.

Before, you decide to pick an auction house to move your merchandise to; you want to attend auctions at the auction house over several weeks. You want to judge the crowd and the average gross sale of the people that are auctioning off their stuff. If this is a great auction house, you will see the same sellers over and over again and many members of the crowd will be regulars.

If you see new people every week and you note that the sales are not that great, then you have your answer whether or not you will use this auction house as a resale channel. Many other things will emerge from this research—you will find out how the auction house does business; you will see how well or not the vendors are treated. You'll learn payment policies and payout policies. A larger auction house usually will pay you within 30, up to 60 days. You will be required to sign a contract stating that you have read, understand and agree to these terms. Smaller auction houses typically pay out that night after they take out their fee, which usually runs 15%–25% on top of a "spot fee" which you pay the auction house for granting you the right to sell your stuff at their auction.

Life is what you make it!

Be very savvy and pay attention to these fees. If you run a low margin storage auction unit through the auction house, after you subtract unit cost, labor, fuel, lodging, food and the spot fee, you may not be making that much money. One of the most fundamental things of any business is learning to watch your metrics or some would say "numbers like a hawk".

As a business person, you should know whether you're making money are losing money on a daily basis. By monitoring this information, you can spot correct; if you wait until the end of the week, or worse, the end of the month, many bad things can happen and you will be unaware of those issues until it is too late.

Should You Use Auction Houses?

This will be a matter of personal preference; there are many people that do not want the responsibility of owning a store. The money that they leave on the table is a small price to pay compared to the price that they would pay by being a store proprietor. I can say many people are not cut out for store ownership. Having your own business that includes a store is a huge responsibility. The factors that come into play—in making the decision to use an auction house—should be based on the personal goals that you set for yourself. Learn to think long term and strategically; being seduced by the quick buck can leave you penniless years later, if you are not careful.

A huge factor to consider will be the availability of auction houses. Every town and city will not be in possession of an auction house. If there's not one to sell at, your decision's made. Maybe, if you are an enterprising storage auction buyer, you can create your own auction house. You will need a building, permits and a licensed auctioneer. If you cannot find a licensed auctioneer, you can attend auctioneer school yourself and run the house and auctions. I know quite a few people that have done this. So, not only are you making money off of your stuff, you are collecting spot fees and commission from the sale of other peoples stock. I have thought about it on many occasions, there were just too many things going on for me to devote my time and attention to it. I know quite a few auctioneers; most of them are really funny and great people to be around. It's a wonderful profession and licensed auctioneers that know how to market well, make a great income.

Life is what you make it!

13

Gold Diamonds & Iron

As a professional storage auction buyer, there's a very good chance that you will come across gold, silver, platinum and diamonds. There are a few rules of engagement when you're trying to sell these items. The first thing is, you must ensure that they are real. Gold is easy to determine; there is an acid test that is sold on eBay which usually runs $25.00–$30.00. What you will do is take the item in question, rub it on a stone block and apply the appropriate acid 10K, 14K 18K or 22K on the gold (hopefully) residue that is left on the stone. If it dissolves, it ain't gold! I have seen a great deal of gold in my own storage auction career. I can eyeball gold with a 95% accuracy rate. Gold has a certain look and more importantly, **"feel"** to it. A real gold chain will be heavier than a fake gold chain that is a little larger. Gold is actually a heavy metal and it does not corrode. These are some signs that you have fake gold or less than karat gold **(less than Karat gold is real gold mixed with something else—it does not have enough gold content to reach the 10K threshold)**

There's a lot of fake gold out there; the first sign will be the stamp—**10K, 14K, 18K, 22K**— the stamps in real gold are clear and well defined. Even if the stamp is worn away from wear, which happens a lot in wedding bands, it will still be clearer and more defined than the stuff you will see in fake gold. After you've gotten quite a few hauls of gold, you will notice that a few golden rings and chains in the palm of your hand will have quite a bit of weight! I have held $1250.00 worth of gold in the palm of my hand several times. Another sign of fake gold is it looks **"brassy"**. There is a lot of costume jewelry out there that is very well made and looks real but it will not have a stamp on it and it has that brassy look. Real gold will not corrode, pit, stain or flake and when it is broken, the inside color will match the outside color, unless it is really, really dirty. When in doubt, check it out with the acid testing kit. In the beginning, you will be testing everything because you will not know what to look for, which is a good policy.

It doesn't take much for a few pieces of gold to turn an OK unit into an outstanding unit. Believe it or not, I have gotten more real gold out of units that I bought in the **"hood"** than at any other neighborhood. You will want to check all of your jewelry; many women who have a lot of costume jewelry, will often have a few pieces of real gold, such as a ring or a pair of earrings. If you get one or two pieces of gold out of every third or fourth unit that you bought and you bought 20 units a month, that will be an extra $600–$2000. Many variables come into play such as size, karat and of course how many women's units that you buy.

The vast majority of the gold I obtained came out of units that had a heavy female presence. It did not matter if it was a single woman or a married woman, if most of the items in the unit were those of the woman in a relationship, there were many times that I received a lot of gold out of those types of units. When you get it out of a storage auction unit, just put it in a jar or a pouch and wait until the end of the month to see how much you collect. You'll be amazed, if you are a heavy volume storage auction buyer, how much gold you will come across. My gold resell connection and I would meet every month when I was in the business. The worst month that I ever had with him, was about $900 for the gold that I sold to him and the best month was $6900— and most of that gold that I sold him, came from one person. She was from Egypt and she had gold coming out of her ears! Another source of gold is old computer boards, it is work but you can pull several grams of gold out of a unit full of old computers.

Silver

Real silver, sterling silver or .925 silver is very easy to identify, it will tarnish, and sometimes the silver that you'll find will be black. There are several silver cleaners on the market; all you have to do is dip the silver in the solution and it comes out beautiful. Unfortunately, it becomes much harder when you're dealing with sterling silver serving pieces— with all of the nooks and crannies, you usually you have to clean those by hand and it is a **bitch!**

Silver prices and the price of scrap silver is dependent on volume—you need a lot of silver to make a lot of money. You can always sell it as a jewelry item, but if you collect a lot, it can be a big payday. You will come across a lot of silver and faux silver jewelry. I found a good way to liquidate all of my silver jewelry was to put it in a huge lot, put it on a scale and weigh it, and then sell it on eBay, with titles such as these: **"100 pounds of Costume Jewelry"** or **"35 Pounds of Sterling and Costume Jewelry"** —you get the picture. I would start the bidding off at 99¢ with a fixed shipping price to the continental 48 states. I would offer to ship to the other two states for an additional fee. Let's talk about selling like that today, do not put these lots up at .99 cents! To protect yourself, start the auction off at $9.99 if it is 10 pounds of jewelry and add an additional $10.00 per additional 10 pounds.

Many people that love arts and crafts will be very interested in your jewelry lot. They can use the costume jewelry and silver as raw materials to make something else—it's the ultimate in recycling. Flea market sellers, boutique owners, small businesses and essentially anyone that has a business that resells other items, will be interested in a huge jewelry lot. I sold each and every one and made a very good profit. This is a method to move all of those little pieces of jewelry that you'll start to accumulate.

Platinum

Platinum is an expensive metal and a pain in the butt; it usually comes in the form of an engagement ring—a small sized engagement ring. I sold all of my platinum rings on eBay. This requires a different type of tactic. All the people I sold rings to— we spoke to each other on the phone. **This was my pitch—"you don't know me and you do not know if this ring is real, so let's do this. You go through the phone book and call up any appraiser in Atlanta and I will take the ring to that person. They will call you and give you the appraised value—the fee for the appraisal will come out of my pocket".** Hook, line and

sinker! All of the people were impressed that I gave them a choice of appraiser; for me to be a fraud with a fake ring, I would have to enlist the help of every appraisal service in town. This method will work like a charm on any high value item that you sell online. I never ever utilized the services of an escrow company. I did come across other platinum items, but for the most part, it was rare.

Diamonds

The secondary market for diamonds is not for the faint at heart. The marketing lesson for you is— diamonds are not rare! Not at all, this is why the secondary market sucks. The reason people think diamonds are rare is DeBeers. Way back when, before there was TV, they began this extreme marketing campaign, "diamonds are forever" which came about because of the durability and hardness of diamonds. This is a true feature of diamonds but what is not true is, diamonds are not rare—in some parts of the world they're literally sprinkled across the ground. This just goes to show you the power of a great marketing campaign. You could walk up to a woman and slap her across the face with the statistics that show the diamonds are not uncommon, and she would foolishly dismiss you because in her heart of hearts, she knows it is true.

OK, you now have the diamond in your possession, or what you think to be a diamond. The cheap method to ascertain if the diamond is real and worth anything is to take it to your local pawn shop. They will inform you of its true value within seconds. Do not sell the ring to the pawnshop! Once you know its value, you can begin to market it. Your first round of customers will be people that know you well and trust you. If that does not work, you can sell diamond rings on eBay; your job will be to convince people that they are real.

Use the pick your appraiser method to move the ring. If the scrap gold value is more than you can get in a resale environment, just knock the diamonds out and sell the gold. I will tell you, selling precious metals and stone, if you are not a jewelry store, will be challenging! People will be immediately suspicious. If you consign the jewelry, you will be given up to 50% of the value and more than likely, you would have gotten more money for the scrap value.

Getting Fancy!

If you come across a significant diamond ring, some of it being a carat or more, have it appraised. Here are some tricks that you can use to extract value out of the jewelry that you find. One of the most wonderful things about real gold and precious stones is that you can turn it into something else. Say you don't want to sell it or you can't get your price. Hold onto it, jewelry does not take up a lot of room. If you're a guy, and you have a girl, you can have a special engagement ring made for her. If you are a girl, and you do not like the design of the jewelry, you can make something special for yourself. Be creative, there's a lot that you can do with these items. You can use them to barter for services, merchandise or favors. The world is your oyster, **you just Gotta crack it!**

Copper, Aluminum, Iron, Steel

The names may sound dull, but if you get any one of these metals in a great quantity, you can make substantial money on scrap metals. Many contractors use storage units as their warehouses. In the case of electricians, heating and air contractors, fabricators and ironworkers, they tend to use things in the course of their business that contains these metals.

During my second year in the storage auction business, I bought a unit that had household furniture in the front and several huge spools of copper cable. These spools were so big, I could not roll one on the truck by myself. What is really funny about that buy was I really did not know what I had. I almost threw it away. I was at the dump and I was cleaning out the truck, a guy that was disposing of yard rubbish saw the copper and said, with this incredible look on his face, "**ARE YOU THROWING ALL THAT COPPER AWAY?**" I straighten up real quick and told him no. I almost threw away **$4000**; yes, that is what I got for the copper at the recycling plant. When you bring that much metal in, you do not get cash, they send you a check. When you think of making money with scrap metal, think in terms of volume, you will need a lot for it to be worth your time. As you can see, you virtually can make money with anything that you pull out of a storage unit.

14

Using Consignment Stores?

I am often asked are consignment shops a good place to use as a sales channel for the merchandise that you obtain out of storage units bought at auctions.

The answer is, it depends. I have a very good friend that I admire and respect, who owns a consignment shop. She's very professional and exceptionally good at what she does. The thing that you must understand with a consignment shop is that they are picky. She educates me on what she and her peers are looking for to consign. The items that they accept for consignment should be less than two years old, clean, current style and wrinkle free.

We have already run into a few issues; the vast majority of clothing that you pull out of storage auction units, will be wrinkled and you really do not know if they are dirty or clean. To solve that question, you must wash everything.

Hold up! Is this a current item? Is this less than two years old? What I am telling you is, you can do a great deal of work and you could waste a lot of time on items that will not be accepted by a consignment shop.

To save yourself some time and trouble, most consignment shops have a list of the items that they're looking for, by name brand, that will help you to some degree. I am not saying that it is a bad idea to take stuff to consignment shops; it is something that you need to have a plan and a method to accomplish profitably. Most of the items that you will obtain will not fit their criteria for selling. Consignment shops want current fashions or on the other side, vintage fashions. You may get a piece or two of clothing that fits their criteria. In some cases, everything in the unit will be able to be sold at a consignment shop. If you will use consignment shops as your main selling channel, you will have to get a super deal on every unit that you buy.

A consignment shop will get 50% of the sale so unless you have bought your storage auction unit super cheap, believe or not you now have overhead! The cost of the unit and the fuel that you used to transport the items, are hard costs. If you paid too much for the unit or it is one of those low margin units, you may not be able to afford a 50% consignment fee! This was my method of determining if an item that I had was consignment store worthy.

The unit that the items came out of, if **I was well into the profit zone already, it did not matter if I took a 50% hit!** If I have something that fits the parameters of a consignment shop on hand and I really did not want that item in my store, I would take it on over. If I got the item that I want to take to the consignment shop for free, at that point I could sell it all for the 50% commission because I had absolutely no overhead on that item.

I bought a unit with dozens, hundreds or even thousands of the same items. One of the rules of selling is, if you have two, three or five of more of the same exact item, you only retail one of those items at a time. If the customer feels that they have forever to make a decision, they will.   By only placing one of those items out at a time, you give your customers a compelling reason to make a decision to purchase. So it makes sense to take some of those items to a consignment shop. **The real question should be, can you afford to take those items to a consignment shop?**

FAQ's

Will I need a business license?

There are many things that go into answering the question. The first answer, if you are opening up a store you will need a business license and a certificate of occupancy. If you continue this work out of your home, in some jurisdictions —yes, in other jurisdictions—no. If you start off part–time, I would not even worry about the business license until your business grows. Check with your local department of revenue about their business license requirements for your municipality.

How much money can I make?

This question depends upon your resources, and the amount of free time that you have. I'll give you two examples, I have a stay at home mom who is a student of my webinar. She works the business part time, and she makes $600 to $800 per month. I have a retired executive who had ample resources and jumped right into the business. His gross revenues are in excess of $10,000 per month after nine months of being in the business. In a word, it really depends on where you are in your life. The stay at home mom is, as she says, **"tickled pink at her earnings."**

Life is what you make it!

Do I need a truck?

Yes! You need a truck or access to a truck to pick up your units. Vans and larger SUV's will also work, with the aid of a trailer.

What is the biggest thing you have seen in a unit?

An antique fire truck, that Vince paid $7000.00.

What is the most money that you made off of a storage auction unit?

$62,000.00

What is the strangest thing you ever found in a unit?

A voo doo shrine.

How long did it take you to start making money in the storage auction business?

One week.

What are the best neighborhoods to get the best units?

You can buy a great unit in any neighborhood! Never forget that!

How long were you in the business?

8 years.

Why did you shut down your business?

For many years, I wanted to be a writer of short stories and books. It is a burning desire that is within me that I could not resist any longer. A strange and unfortunate chain of events occurred—I guess you could call it serendipity that allowed me to pursue my dream. I became ill and could no longer run the business. My partner also became ill and later on was diagnosed with cancer. Neither one of us was in a position to continue on. So, I liquidated everything in the warehouse and we shut the business down. Then I began to write, the day was July 17th, 2009 and here we are!

Check out my other books — Glendon Sells Books!

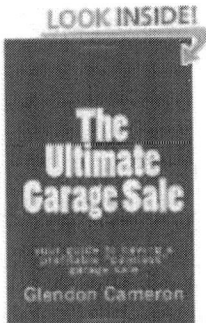

The Ultimate Garage Sale (Volume 1) - **Paperback (Sept. 1, 2010) by Glendon Cameron**

Buy new: **$24.95**

Books: See all 4 items

Life is what you make it!

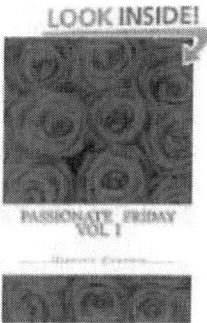

Passionate Friday VOL I: Sensually Spoken (Volume 1) - Paperback (Dec. 21, 2009) by Glendon Cameron

Buy new: **$12.50**

Books: See all 4 items

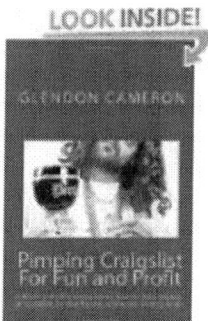

Pimping Craigslist For Fun and Profit: A down and dirty overview on how to make money on craigslist, by buying and selling pre-owned items (Volume 1) - Paperback (Oct. 1, 2010) by Glendon Cameron

Buy new: **$24.99**

Life is what you make it!

Books that will drop in 2011

The Art of Failure

Passionate Friday VOL II

The Porn Is Always In The DVD Player

to stay on top of things subscribe to my blog-
www.urbanpackrat.com or my YouTube channel
www.youtube.com/Glendon007

Life is what you make it!

About the Author

Glendon Cameron is an entrepreneur with over eight years in the storage auction business. After a few years of trial and error, he was able to turn a cottage industry and hidden "business" into a highly profitable full time endeavor. Not many people are aware of the hidden profit potential that the storage auction business delivers. He is about to change all of that!

He has attended over 3000 auctions and bought well over 1250 storage auction units. In 2002, he got started part time and built the business up to a 10,000 square foot resale store, selling everything from appliances to Gucci shoes! He is the nations leading storage auction expert, with the number one storage auction book on Major Online Book Seller.

Glendon grew up in Adamsville, Alabama and is a proud veteran of the United States Army. He lives in a suburb of Atlanta, Georgia.

There is no end of the road if you blaze your own path.......

Life is what you make it!

Notes

Notes

Notes

Your Beginning!

Life is what you make it!

10370704R0

Made in the USA
Lexington, KY
18 July 2011